Typhoon Honey

The Only Way Out Is Through

Kris Girrell
Candace Klein Sjogren

For information, contact

MSI Press LLC

1760-F Airline Highway, #203

Hollister, CA 95023

Front cover design: Julie Sorkin-Maguire, www.maguiredesignstudio.com

Back cover design: Opeyemi Opeyemi

Layout & typesetting: Opeyemi Opeyemi

Copyeditor: Lynne Curry

Library of Congress Control Number: 2021911458

ISBN 978-1-950328-96-3

Dedicated:

To Sarah, my spouse, partner, playmate, and travel buddy, who first enrolled me in a transformation program and set my feet on this path. Without your support, encouragement and trust, I would not be here today. To Ray Blanchard, PhD, the trainer who showed me what is possible when we release the stories. Thank you all for this life of joy and abundance.

-   *Kris Girrell, Andover, MA*

To Andrew, Ivar, and August – You inspire me daily to trust, surrender, and play. To Michael Strasner, my mentor, coach, business partner, and friend – Thank you for leading the way for me and so many others. Together, you have each taught me how to create a life worth living.

-   *Candace Sjogren, Jamaica Plain, MA*

Table of Contents

Section One - Physical Foundations of Source

Section Two - Psychological Foundations of Source

Section Three - The Tools of Becoming Source

Section Four - Standing As Source

Section One

*Physical Foundations
of Source*

Kris Girrell & Candace Sjogren

Orientation:
About Our Stories and Case Examples

Welcome to our world! There are two things you should know about our writing in this book. First of all, we (Candace and Kris) will write about our personal experiences in first person. It felt awkward to be talking about ourselves in the third person, and it is our contention that you'll easily determine whose voice is speaking (one of us is a large, aging athletic male, and the other is a much younger executive, female powerhouse of child-bearing age)! Secondly, throughout this book we will make illustrative points by telling stories about people we have known or coached in this work. Every story or case example is created from a combination of actual people one of us knows (and in some cases even includes our own personal experiences). They are illustrative stories that can be used for reference or comparison. The cases are real; however, the names have been changed and the circumstances have been blended across several persons to protect the confidentiality of any individual. Here is a case in point:

Everybody knows Ariana. She's just that type of person—outgoing, successful, and caring. And what they all know, or at least believe, about her is that everything she touches turns to gold. It doesn't hurt matters that she is extremely attractive—outwardly she is strikingly beautiful but inwardly she has an infectiously positive, almost magnetic personality. When you are around her, you just feel better—more positive, more energetic, and more alive. Some say she lives a charmed life; others think that she has a guardian angel or a sugar daddy who helps her out when she's "up against it." But few know her real back story.

Ariana was born to a single teen mother in the backwoods of Arkansas. Her dad was non-existent from shortly after the time of conception, and her mom launched into a series of unhealthy and abusive relationships that continued until fairly recently. One of those "stepfathers" had badly beaten her around the age of nine, an action that had resulted in her being placed under guardianship of the state Child Protective Services and foster homes— "Yes, homes is plural," she'll point out, "nobody stays in one place for long." The last of these settings was a Catholic school run by the Dominican Sisters, which is where she got her first shot at learning self-esteem.

At that point in life, something clicked for Ariana—something inside that that became her grounding and could never be taken away. It wasn't any sort of religion. Rather, it was a sense of believing that she was worth caring for and that she was the one person (perhaps the only one) most capable of taking care of that. Ariana began seeking out opportunities: scholarships to colleges, self-improvement programs, a summer abroad program, and so on. You name it; she went after it. With each experience she grew in stature and skills and yet never lost that sense of humility of knowing from whence she came or the gratitude for the Sisters who had believed in her. The rest, as they say, is history, until the successful woman we see today was born.

During college, Ariana secured an internship at a bank where she learned about investment banking. After graduation, she was hired by the CEO of a start-up company who literally put her in charge of every aspect of the business from finance to marketing and production. With those skills, she was recruited as an assistant to a prominent investment banker. Armed with her "can-do" attitude, skills in writing, years of researching all sides of an issue, and broad knowledge of what it takes to make a business successful, she was quickly promoted. But the pace of the investment banking industry kept her from doing what she really wanted to do—invest in others like herself and pay back the gift. So, after a few years of success as an analyst, Ariana launched out on her own. She moved into a not-for-profit agency and started a program that incubated other young women's businesses. She helped them get funding, run "kick-starts," and get the right advice to make businesses work. Today people refer to her as a beacon of hope for struggling young women. And she has no intention of slowing down.

Yes, everything Ariana touches turns out well (most of the time), but people don't see her failures and flops. She calls them lessons and learns everything she can from those crashes and face-plants. Each lesson makes her smarter and seemingly more successful. She not only doesn't see them as failures, she actually seeks them out and embraces them as the teachable moments that they are. When asked about her attitude, she points out that she never learned anything from winning or from successes—except that whatever she did had worked. But failures, she adds, "failures teach you volumes if you are willing to take them in as yours; as something you created or sourced."

That, friends, is the Ariana difference. And it is the central concept of this book. What Ariana and so many like her (we all know an Ariana somewhere) do is own the idea that everything around them is feedback on how they have created these results, positive or negative. Most of us are proud of our successes and quick to claim responsibility. However, just as many of us are quick to identify the external forces that seemed to have resulted in our failures rather than to use them as feedback on our own way of being.

The latter is not our view. In reality, we do not view events or feedback as either positive or negative. Feedback is just information. The idea that things are good or bad, positive or negative, can severely hinder our progress in this journey. So from this point forward, you will find us referring to situations as either advancing our movement or serving as corrective and constructive information.

Typhoon Honey is a book about creating an "unprecedented" future of success and joy (as in, creating a future with no *preceding* evidence that it is possible). It involves some of the above (taking and integrating feedback), but it is a tad more complicated. In looking at the Ariana story or others like her, what we fail to see are the hours and days of work and dedication, the many—far too many—times she had to pick herself up and go back at it. This is a practiced way of being that works in harmony with the forces around us, including other people (all people, not just friends), physical forces (like the laws of physics) and invisible forces and energies, to maximize our contribution to the world in return. This book is neither delusional nor mythical. It is realistic (though we will be redefining that term as part of our exploration) and practicable.

To understand how this all works and understand your part in creating an unprecedented future, we will begin laying a foundation of some core principles that operate in the world around us. Section 1 delves into how the world, the universe, we as individuals, and even the laws of the universe are all connected. It places us in the middle of real, physical factors that can either work for us or against us depending on our awareness of them. It is imperative that we understand how these laws and boundaries function in order to be able to work in harmony with them instead of struggling against them.

The second section digs deeply into the psychological nature of perceptions and challenges you to rethink how you understand reality. We will take a peek at how our defenses can get in the way of doing this work. While ego defenses are protective, they often get out of control and separate us from others. Our defenses, driven by our natural fears and insecurities, result in our isolating and moving away from the very people who we love and need the most.

Section three explores what we call our "circumstances" or the "reality" of our current situation. In this section you will begin to question the certainty or immutable nature of some of your current situations. Here we will lay out a set of tools we use and practice when becoming the source of our lives.

Section four takes on the whole concept of being the source and soul author of your life. From this place of personal ownership and accountability, we delve into how being the sole author of your life works and how to stay fully rooted in the practices. It is not our belief that anyone can maintain perfection in living as the source and author of one's life, but with practice one can get fairly good at it.

This book is meant to be a dialogue. We will offer exercises throughout each section and with each new concept we introduce. We encourage you to purchase a notebook and to not only complete the exercises as they are laid out, but to journal your journey through the process. Some who are reading this are already accomplished and have a great life they want to take to the next level, while others may be new to this type of lifestyle. But even those who are already practicing becoming the source of their lives and just leveling up will find it valuable to journal along with the exercises. We always like to say that a life worth living is a life worth writing about. Please note that some of the exercises will feel counterintuitive, which they are! The exercises are meant to stretch your skills and ways of being, and quite truthfully, if they were intuitively obvious, you would already be doing them. Some of the exercises are simple tasks and others—the tougher ones, perhaps—are set apart in shaded boxes as separate exercises beyond the text.

If your copy of *Typhoon Honey* is a paper version of the book, we encourage you to write in the margins, highlight sections and key thoughts, and make notes you can refer back to. If you have purchased an electronic version of it, you will find hyperlinks throughout the text. These will allow you to move forward and back as well as links to outside resources and articles. We will also provide a link to the authors' contact information to send us your own experiences and stories. Your stories will be blended with others and added into the next editions of the book so that we can continue to show how these tools really work.

But why the title of *Typhoon Honey*? Pacific Ocean typhoons are typically much larger than their Atlantic cousins, called hurricanes. The force of the wind and the massive area they map out make typhoons one of nature's wonders. While typhoons can be quite destructive, it is their force and power that we hold in awe. Inside the vortex often large things can be crushed or hurtled helter-skelter like little pieces of paper. But, what if, in the midst of this power, we found the sweetest delight known to our kind? Honey.

Honey is one of the oldest known sources of food (and perhaps delight). Even before written history, cave drawings from over eight thousand years ago refer to finding and gathering honey. Honey is clear and glistening in the sun. Honey is sweet and sticky and you don't even mind the mess! And honey is the only food source known that does not spoil or mold. Honey is a gift from the gods!

Juxtaposing these two thoughts seems oxymoronic indeed. But that is exactly what living your life as the source of it all is like. It is living in a life of what we call "both/and"—not a life of either/or where you have to choose one thing over another. Living as the source of your future and present means having it all—choosing to have both this and that. Like seeing that in spite of the storms around us, we can still find sweet honey in the moment.

That's one way of explaining this strange title. But there is another.

Typhoon Honey is actually the name of a tour guide we met in Saigon. We don't know if that was his given name or if he just made it up. But Typhoon Honey was irresistible. He was short and almost as round as he was tall, and he had an infectious giggle type of laugh with which he punctuated every sentence. His outlook on life was joyous, and it was so clear that he loved every person he met, without reserve or judgment. You'll meet up with Typhoon Honey later on in this book, but for now, let's just say that this one man so embodied the life of joy and abundance that we will be discussing throughout this book that we could not resist the urge to name it in his honor. His very way of being caused others to be pulled in. In the book we describe what we call "standing as source"—a way of being that causes your life to be the way it is. Typhoon Honey was the source; he drew people in, he created joy, he held no judgments and everything around him was sweet and delicious!

Thank you for joining us on this journey. We hope that you will find it to be the key to a life of exciting abundance and to spreading love, passion, and connection to the others in your life.

Everything Is Connected

It is critically important to make this point right from the start: the tools of transformation are not practiced in a vacuum. Everything in this book and everything that you learn in a transformational program is part of a greater whole. If you try to do some of the "tricks" and techniques without a realization that you are a physical being living in a physical world, or that you are a psychological being dealing with other psychological entities (people), you will be sorely disappointed. We are all functioning inside of this greater whole called a cosmos and work within that reality. It is important to keep these "realities" forefront in your thinking and to use them as part of your "being," as in the way you are being (not doing)—not that you could deny them if you would want to. This all works together.

Judith was a successful business woman who had grown her company and successfully sold it off realizing a great profit. It seemed wonderful as she now could take her family on long vacations exploring many wonderful parts of the world. On the surface she looked to be the picture of success. But she came into a transformational program seeking answers. Without her old role and company, she felt lost and didn't know where to take her career. Her marriage was in disrepair and she was actually considering divorce. And most of all, she was unhappy.

Throughout the program she kept saying she wanted to fix things, but she did not see any connection between the various parts of her life and the tools presented in her transformation program. In the leadership level of her program, she was quite successful at driving the project. She successfully enrolled her husband in the program. And she even got started on a new job and career. But she was unwilling to view her life holistically. So, when the program ended, she phoned her coach to complain that "it didn't work." She was willing to admit that she had "half-assed" her way through the program. She hadn't used all of the tools, choosing some that fit her world view and discarding others she saw as not fitting her. Judith half-asses her way in everything and she finally saw the effects of that style of operation. It simply doesn't deliver powerful and unprecedented results. The program had not worked because Judith had not worked the program.

This book cannot deliver answers. Yes, this is a self-help book, and certainly we will be presenting many great tools, asking that you work each of them as we go through them. But *you* own the responsibility for understanding these two principles from the outset:

1. Nothing really happens unless you put in the effort. It is up to you to make these principles and practices work for you through your effort and practice.

2. You absolutely understand that life is "whole cloth." Things are not separate compartments that have no interrelatedness with the rest of the world and the rest of your life. And perhaps, mvost importantly, that all of this (you, your life, your network of friends, family and coworkers, the country, the world and the universe) is a huge system of connected parts on one great whole. So we will begin there.

We cannot escape our interconnectedness, just as we cannot escape our physical nature. It was not that long ago, historically speaking, that science and philosophy (along with its two children, theology and psychology) were both seeking answers to our existence. How did we come to be? How did we begin and evolve to be like this? Both explored the world of questions, but they eventually parted company when religion claimed absolutism and science still questioned it. In the hundred years between Copernicus (1473-1543) and Galileo (1564-1642) the church retreated into a fundamentalist view that resulted in both the Inquisition and Galileo's house confinement for the remainder of his years. Religion/philosophy and science were fully separated, a fate they both suffered until just recently.

The unfortunate consequence of that division was that science went down one path and the understanding of humans, our beingness and purpose, down another. It was not until recently that these two divorced partners have begun speaking with each other again. We are finally entering an age where the students of psychology are looking to research in science to answer the great philosophical questions of how we evolved, how we function, and how we are integrally entwined with the forces of the universe. As it turns out, there is a lot to unpack here—far more than the scope of this book. But we want to bring a few of those intersections to light in this discussion.

Recent studies in astrophysics have discovered two important realities about our universe: First, the fabric of space is not empty and void. Second, this universe and all of its billions of galaxies and their innumerable stars and planetary systems is a complete and interconnected whole, every part of which is acting and reacting to the movements and forces of every other part. Not only are we "not alone" in the universe, we are inextricably a part of it and affected by it. In this section we will deal with only a tiny subset of that interactive dynamic—the parts that we can perceive more readily. Our request is that you trust the science of it all.

You and I are physical beings and, as such, act and react according to the laws of physics, not simply physically but emotionally and spiritually as well. Take gravity for an example. When was the last time you defied gravity? We recognize that gravity—the magnetic pull of the earth— keeps us tethered to this planet. So in much the same way, all of the laws of physics and the physical world apply to us.

We are connected not simply to the planet and to the forces of the moon that orbits the planet (the moon that causes tides in our oceans and in our bodies, which are also mostly water), but to the forces within ourselves and those around us. Think of a time when you *felt* someone enter the room before you saw them. Did you notice that the energy changed? Some people add life and sparkle, while others seem to suck the oxygen and life out of the room. Have you ever felt someone's eyes were on you without actually seeing them? People have and exude energy. It is fairly simple to see the energy around people with the use of instruments that detect subtle wave lengths and outputs.[1] So it is only logical to extrapolate that these energies also interact with other people's energies.

But "everything is connected" goes well beyond that. Researchers have found that even if they split an atom, sending each part in different directions hundreds of miles away, actions (like passing through a magnetic field) on one part of the now-split atom result in the identical reaction on the other part more than a hundred miles away. Scientists call this phenomenon *quantum entanglement*, and it happens on all levels of the physical world. This means that, as humans, we are also "entangled" on some quantum level. Studies have been done (and replicated) where a group of people meditating and focusing their energy on a petri dish in a lab a thousand miles away have a profound effect on the growth of the culture in the dish. Focusing positive or negative energy on water (first demonstrated in the 90s by Japanese researcher, Masaru Emoto) affected the shape of the frozen crystals of the water.[2] In other words, our thoughts are connected to physically observed results ("realities," if you will).

The scientific community was skeptical of the claims of Emoto's study, so researchers at Stanford University conducted a triple-blind study in 2008[3] using 1,900 people in Germany who focused their intentions on water samples in an energetically sealed room in California. The results were evaluated by a group of 2,500 judges who were completely unaware of the purpose of the study. Judges consistently noted a slight to significant difference in the beauty of the crystals in the study over the control samples. These and so many other examples of quantum entanglement happen around us on a regular basis and serve as further substantiation of the interconnectivity of all things. Based on these and other studies, we posit that our thoughts

---

1 Barbara Ann Brennan, *Hands of Light: A Guide to Healing Through the Human Energy Field*. (New York: Bantam Books, 1988). Brennan was an atmospheric physicist at NASA's Goddard Space Flight Center when she discovered that the instruments used in sensing deep space energetic patterns could reveal the energetic patterns around people when aimed at them.

2 Masaru Emoto, *The Hidden Messages in Water*. (New York: Atria Books, 2006, originally published in Japanese by Sunmark Publishing in 2001). Emoto was a businessman and neither a scientist nor a medical doctor who was widely criticized by the scientific community until the replication studies corroborated his theories.

3 Dean Radin et al., "Effects of Distant Intention on Water Crystal Formation: A Triple Blind Replication," *Journal of Scientific Exploration* 22, no. 4, (2008): 481-493,

and intentions have an interactive effect on the physical world around us. Your being, your presence, your thoughts and the world around you are all connected.

We are connected even more deeply than just our quantum entanglement. You and I (and in fact the entire world that we know of) are created of the same materials—everything is made of the same stuff. As far as our explorations of deep space can tell us, the entire universe is made of the same stuff. We—that is you, me, all humans, the planet, the stars, everything—come from the same infinite source that produced/produces everything. We literally are one with the universe and it is not at all figuratively speaking to say that at our core, we are a part of that one, infinite source.

Jack is a man in his late 70s and is highly educated beyond the PhD level. He has been a professor, teaching other doctoral candidates for most of his later years. He is married with several kids all of whom are successful and married with children as well. He is close to his children and his grandchildren and can connect with his extended family often and whenever he likes. Yet, despite all of this, he is a man who is, in his own words, "waiting to die." Jack is still hung up on a divorce that happened over twenty years ago and has not gotten over it, although his ex-wife is happily married in a loving, committed relationship. His story is that he wasted the best years of his life because his ex at the time of the divorce was an alcoholic. As a result, he has repeatedly convinced himself that his life is over and a waste.

Nowadays, when Jack holds his grandchildren while they giggle and laugh, when he sees his own children in happy, loving relationships, and even when he travels to far-off places (something he says he likes to do) and experiences wonderful tastes in different foods and beautiful scenes, he continues to bring this dark cloud of gloom with him that dampens any of his experiences. His children fear that he actually will die a sour, unhappy man—that this sadness might actually kill him.

Jack is a man who literally could see himself as a part of this universe of abundance and beauty if he chose to. He has the power and the intellect to see how he is inextricably connected to all else in the universe, yet he consciously has decided to separate himself from that world view and hold himself as an example of how alone he really is.

Later in the book, we will be discussing the practice of becoming the source of your life, but bookmark this thought right now. Standing as source (our shorthand way of describing it), being able to cause the life and the abundance you desire, is only possible because you are a part of this infinite source. When you get this one truth—get it on a deep level in your bones—you are able to tap into that source of which you are an elemental part. The only thing that stands between you and having all of that infinite wonderfulness at your disposal is your mind. If you think you are alone and separate from the rest of life, that you are an existential bag of bones and flesh, condemned to your separation from all else, you will be. But if you want to be a part of this grand universal power pack called abundance, you know (not think, not believe, but *know*) that you are a part of the infinite abundance of the universe. Achieving that level of awareness is what we call transformation.

Defining Transformation

The nature of everything in this world we know of and in which we live is change. Nothing is static and immutable—nothing. Neither concrete buildings nor stones. Not mountains nor oceans. Nothing lasts forever without changing. Not only is everything in a constant state of flux (though admittedly at different rates and speeds), but the nature of those changes is purely chaotic. The universe is chaos that moves in patterned forms which we call fractals (self-repeating patterns). So when we begin to talk about change and what change is, we start with the idea that change is natural and continual.

This is no new concept. The ancient sages observed changes happening around them and sought to understand the nature of change and changing systems more than three thousand years ago. The "Book of Changes," called the *I Ching*, is probably the most widely known of the systems for understanding change. Presumably compiled somewhere between 800 and 1000 BCE by Lao Tzu, the *I Ching* breaks down change into three phases (start, middle and finish) in eight different combinations, each of which could have a yin aspect or a yang aspect. For purposes of this discussion, let's refer to them as a strong/hard aspect and a gentle/receptive aspect. These were represented as a solid bar or a broken bar.

Combining those two possibilities across the eight combinations produced the 64 elements of the *I Ching*. While simple in its design, what the *I Ching* represents is that we humans have been trying to understand change for well over three thousand years.

We don't have to look back to the sages, however, to recognize how present change is in our lives. We enter this world as a change. The last stage of the birthing process is called "transition" because we change states from fetus to infant. From infant we change to crawling to toddler and so on. All of us as adults underwent a significant change (whether we liked it or not) in puberty when the hormones of our bodies shaped us into the form we see today. And scientists tell us that we lose about 7,000-10,000 skin cells every time we shower. We slough off cells, alter our physiques, and lose or grow hair. To be alive means to be changing.

Nothing is constant except for change! When we discuss change, we will be referring to those normal types of changes external to us and internal to us, with which we adapt and get comfortable.

That said, as working adults you also know that organizational change is hard to accomplish and the source of much confusion. There are two simple reasons why change, and in particular organizational change, is difficult. The first is relatively obvious in the term organization. The nature of an organization is, well, organized. Changing that organizational structure is difficult. Depending on the rigidity of the organization and the number of years it has existed in a certain form, it can be quite difficult to achieve, just on the level of the organizational structure itself. But the second reason why change is experienced as difficult is that each individual experiences change uniquely and personally—each time.

Contrary to popular belief, we don't really resist change as humans (as is the commonly held belief). Our brains resist change. Much like the organization, our brain's sole function is to make order out of chaos (given that the world around us is a whirling, chaotic change system). The brain's job is to take that disorder and chaos and classify it, name it and categorize it so that we can then function within it and navigate through the changes. Our brain has been doing that since birth so it gets pretty good at mastering the chaos around it. Our brains have even created the organizations we work in, the infrastructures we use to get to work, our tools and the Internet and everything we employ to manage it all. So, when a change comes along that disrupts the nicely ordered mental models we have built, our brains throw a fit! But after it is done rebelling against the change, it goes right back to work figuring out that change and creating some method for understanding how to deal with that change.

We all have seen the news story when a tornado rips through some midwestern town, leveling everything in a half-mile wide swath of destruction. Invariably the news team is on the scene in a flash to interview the people who have been affected. Often, we see two different families being interviewed. The first family is huddled together tearfully surveying the rubble that used to be their house. "We lost everything," they say through the tears, "There is nothing left, nothing for us to do; we just don't know what we will do or where we will go from here." Just down the street, the crew interviews a second family. Mama is stroking her child's face as she smiles. Her husband and their teenage daughter are beside them holding hands. "We are so grateful," he says, "None of us was hurt. We may have lost the house, but we have each other and that is what counts. We are blessed!" Change affects us all in some way—even when it is pure havoc and destruction. How we make sense of it is something we will be addressing throughout this book.

If, then, we were to define change, *it would be some event or process that challenges the status quo of our current understanding and coping mechanisms.* Change causes us to rethink and reconfigure how we are going to deal with different circumstances. Change is normal. Resistance to change is normal, unique, personally defined and—wait for it—to be expected. There is nothing wrong with how we deal with changes that needs to be "fixed." All we need to do is understand what is changing, what is being affected within our world, and then get practiced at shifting with each subsequent change. But change is not transformation, nor is transformation change.

Transformation, as we will be using it in this book, is a deep disruption or rearrangement of the core beliefs we hold which direct how we live our life in this world. Transformation consists of two roots: *Trans*, which means movement across or from one place to another or one state to another, and *formation*, which is about how our self-concept is formed. We think of formation as it is described in the "formative years" in developmental psychology. What is "formed" is the essence of our personality and our ways of being. This takes place through our experiences and the interpretations we make about ourselves because of those experiences. In other words, the idea of "self" is formed one layer and one experience at a time.

Given that backdrop, transformation is the process of shifting our inner self concepts from one previously held way of knowing ourselves to a new and different way of being. Transformation, however, is not the process of becoming something that you are not already. Rather, transformation involves rediscovering that purest you that you were meant to be. It can be thought of as a systematic delayering of that which is in the way of your becoming that authentic, true self you were meant to be.

Change and transformation are two distinctly different processes. Pop psychology and contemporary usage seem to blend the two terms together or see them as interchangeable. Change, doing things differently or dealing with differing challenges, is relatively easy to understand and teach. We have been teaching change management for decades and have easy-to-understand templates and processes for teaching individuals and managers how to deal with change.

Little however has been done to make sense of transformation. Human transformation programs like EST, Lifespring, Insight, Landmark Education, Ascension Leadership, Next Level Trainings and the Boston Breakthrough Academy employ trainers who have literally decades of training on how to support people in the difficult and challenging process of transformation. It is not a subject that we take lightly nor is it something that is easily accomplished. In the pages that follow, we will be discussing difficult subjects that are not generally discussed in self-help books. There are only two forces in the world that are strong enough to cause transformation: *unconditional love and deep suffering.*

Learning to be totally unconditional in loving is a tall order. Unconditional means just that: there are no conditions placed on who gets to be loved. If and when you get to a place of unconditional love, you see into the pure soul of each person and see the tender beauty each person has—not some, not just my tribe, but everyone. Practicing unconditional love means loving even the most despicable person that seems to represent the antithesis of everything that you hold sacred and true. That is uncomfortable.

But the other path of transformation, deep suffering, might be even more disquieting. Suffering has the power to rip a person wide open, and in doing so, open their hearts with compassion. Pain and suffering open up a level of understanding of the human condition—that we all feel pain and experience suffering. Neither path is easy. Most programs of human transformation will use both unconditional love and the experience of suffering as the vehicles of transforming the participants.

With that description of transformation, you might ask, "why would anyone sign up for that ride?" It does not sound like fun to be ripped open to vulnerability or to see that you are called to love everyone including *that* person—your worst nightmare! But at the same time, with the right attitude about transformation, it need not be depressing! We personally know many, many people who embrace their pains knowing that what is on the other side of them is a life of unequalled prosperity and joy.

When I first came into the work of transformation, I had just miscarried after several years of infertility and treatments. I was in a great deal of physical and emotional pain and didn't quite know how to transform that. Using the tools of transformation, I started unpacking my sense of suffering and discovered that I had some deep trauma around being molested as a child. I had been avoiding dealing with that for more than thirty-five years! When I began to embrace that trauma and decided to love the perpetrator, I finally was able to let go of the pain and suffering. On the other side of that letting go, I not only found a new level of light and happiness but I was actually able to get pregnant. I was able to transform some heavy and latent pain so that I could actually bring a child into the world.

If you've had dreams of your excellence, they probably come from some sense of the greatness you hold inside. If you have ever thought you could be a star at something wonderful, or a business owner, or a successful entrepreneur, that thought most likely came from some feeling of your inner purpose. We all have that, but it may have been crushed or blotted out by life experiences that told you dreams were foolish. We all were told as kids "stop daydreaming" or "be realistic." And gradually we took on that somber mannerisms of the world of "supposed to" or "should" and began to play small. Transformation is about playing a big game—*your* big game, the one you were meant to play. In accessing your natural capacity to deeply feel and deeply love, you can build the strength and conviction necessary to make dreams a reality.

Brief Exercise:
   Your most fulfilled self is not a wish (like "I wish I could be like Tom Brady" or "I wish I were a billionaire"). It is, however, a deeply held dream. It could be a haunting sense of something greater. The difference is that when you think of your greatest self, you get chills; the hair on the back of your neck stands up! The difference is that wishes are the fantasies of the ego and dreams are expressions of your soul.
   Describe one such dream you have had that is not yet manifested— something you feel you have the potential to become. What is the difference between this and your ego-driven wishes? Complete the picture: With your dream, describe a scene wherein you have begun living your highest purpose. What does it look like? Who is there with you? What does that feel like? Now park that for a moment—we'll revisit your dreams a bit later.

Physics and the Laws of Motion

   Dreams, alone, are ineffective in transforming our lives without having a meaningful relationship with the physical world. "A little less talk. A lot more action," as Elvis sang. We cannot spin gold from straw. We cannot make things happen out of thin air. We need to understand how things work and how we can become part of that grand scheme of all things.
   As we said, we are all physical beings living in a physical world inside of a physical cosmos. As such we are subject to the same physical laws that govern the movement of the stars, the oceans, and even trains. But whereas our laws seem to be made to regulate and adjudicate or, as Thurgood Marshall once wrote, "to prevent, proscribe, and punish, the laws of the universe seem to be focused on connection, attraction, and holding." Isaac Newton is given credit for naming one set of those physical laws—the laws of motion. These three laws are truisms about how movement and stasis work and can easily be observed in our actions, reactions, and movements. They also apply quite nicely to our human development.

Newton's First Law of Motion

An object in motion will stay in motion unless acted on by an external force.

Without the forces of gravity or friction, objects would stay in perpetual motion. However, they do not because of the continual interaction of these outside forces. When applied to our daily lives, we would continue on our current course (our path, as it were) indefinitely were it not for things that "get in our way." These things range the gamut of our life circumstances from resources, finances, and nutrition, to locomotion (cars and stuff), weather, politics, and wars (including both the existence or the lack of any of these factors). Your life, the beating of your heart, and your ability or inability to walk and move about are all essentially bodies in motion with some degree of interaction from outside or opposing forces.

What keeps us in motion? Why do we perceive ourselves as moving or as needing to move? Why, when we feel trapped or feel that our movement is stymied, do we feel upset? Furthermore, why are not all humans gifted with the same rate of motion or the same ability to deal with the outside forces and circumstances in their lives?

Newton's Law does not guarantee equality. The law does not care whether it is acting on an animate being or an inanimate object. The actions of physical entities (like us) just act or move.

The corollary to the first law is that any object at rest will tend to stay at rest unless put into motion by some outside force. Ah, now this is the fun stuff! If we are perhaps static, comfortable or just inactive, there are forces that can act on us that will change that. A good swift kick in the pants can stir us into action! But the outside force does not have to be a violent action. It can be gentle or loving and suddenly we find ourselves in motion again. But get this: Our own intention can be that force that puts us into action. Left unchallenged, our inertia will keep us in a state of non-movement.

Scientists call that kick in the pants "activation energy." It is the force required to actually get up out of bed in the morning when you don't want to. I ran four Boston Marathons, and on those winter days when it was nasty outside and everyone I knew was snuggled in their beds, I laced up my sneakers and got out in the darkness and cold and put in the miles. The activation energy in that case consists of two things: one, Pheidippides, the first marathon runner, died after his declaration of "Eureka, we have won!" in Athens because he did not train to run that far, and two, Dana Farber Cancer Institute (for whom I ran) wisely pairs you up with some bald-headed kid who is fighting cancer such that you can no longer whine that you have it bad. Activation energy is a force that can put an inert body into motion in a heartbeat.

We tend, as humans, to pursue our present course through life, assuming that there is no other way—it is what it is. We may think, "I was born into poverty, and there is little to nothing I can do to break out of that." Or perhaps another holds the belief that she is smart, or not smart enough, or good looking or not. Whatever the case, our physical experience of these life issues is that it is a train on the tracks, an action or inaction put into play about which we have no control. But intention and will are forces that can and often do propel us into another dimension at a new and drastically different rate of motion! We'll get there; but for now, let's continue with the laws of motion.

Newton's Second Law of Motion

Force equals mass times acceleration.

Growing up we noticed that big things seem to have a big impact and smaller things less so. Small plows can move small amounts of material, but gigantic bulldozers can move mountains of dirt.

Newton also observed the opposite to be true; that small things can have huge impacts under the right condition. This equation observes that a small and perhaps light object can, if or when accelerated, penetrate or overpower a much larger and seemingly tougher object. A piece of straw can embed itself into a tree trunk when accelerated by the force of a tornado. A small projectile the size of a pin, when shot at the speed of sound, will create a force called a shock wave that will blow a significant hole in a wood plank. And a five-foot-ten running back can hit the line with such explosive power that he knocks the six-foot-six 375-pound defensive lineman backwards. $f=m^*a$.

Applied to our human world, this translates to the fact that even a small action or deed with significant acceleration will move mountains. $F=ma$

means that it is the acceleration with which the deed or even the thought is attempted that determines the force of its impact—not its size. So just what might that accelerator be? For our purposes, the accelerator is your intention. Intentionality is neither wishful thinking nor is it a kind of probability estimate.

Often when we think about our intention to do something, we consider the risk/reward structure and the overall probability of success we might have. But what we mean by intention here has more to do with your clarity and focus than any outside and interfering "forces." Things start to happen once you become clear about your intent. Stuff that you had never noticed suddenly appears almost serendipitously. In actuality, those things had been there all along, but it was not until we became focused and intent that we were able to notice them and take advantage of them.

It is somewhat akin to what we call the "new car syndrome." Let's say you have always driven a Toyota Camry, but on your latest excursion to the dealer, she suggested trying out a new Avalon (a slightly larger and more luxurious version of the Camry). You tell the saleswoman that you had never heard of an Avalon and didn't know Toyota made such a vehicle, but it's love at first sight and you buy it. But here's the wrinkle: on the way home from purchasing your new light green Avalon, you notice not one, but eight or ten Toyota Avalons, all in the same color and style despite having never heard of or seen one before that day! The truth is that those cars had always been on the road but until your focus was shifted you had never noticed them. And that is just one of the many aspects of intention as an accelerator.

Physics is physics, and if a law is true in one place, it therefore is true in all other places and applications or it is not a law.

Newton's Third Law of Motion

For every action there is an equal and opposite reaction.

This is the one law of motion that you can most readily identify when doing the work of personal development or transformation. The simple translation of this law is based on the balance of all things in the universe. Just like water seeks to level, the universe seeks balance.

Whenever two bodies interact, they exert a force on each other. When you sit in your chair, for example, notice the feeling of your body exerting a downward force on the chair cushion. But at the same time the chair is exerting an equal and opposite force upward on your bottom to keep you from falling through the floor. Or when swimming, your stroke in the water is a force that seems like you are pushing the water. But without the equal resistance and counteraction of the water in reaction to your stroke, you would stay in the same place. It is the equal and opposite force that propels you through the water. A rocket looks like it is propelled through space because of the power of the flames exploding out of the back of the engine, but it is actually the reactive forces of the exploding gasses inside the engine that propel the rocket forward. Forces always come in pairs.

In much the same way, our development—say our muscular development—does not simply come from movement, but rather from the resistance of an equal and opposite force, the weight being lifted. Running happens when the action of our foot and leg muscles are met by the friction of the track and the gravitational force of the earth.

Applied to personal development and transformation, the equal and opposite action becomes even more powerful and evident. We do not develop when things are going our way; that's just a nice day! We develop when we meet adversity. We all know this to be true.

Think of a tough situation you once had and remember the lesson of that experience. We frequently work with executives and leaders and have them create what we call a "shadow resume." Your regular resume consists of all the nifty results you have created as part of your career experiences, listed as bullet points under each role. But your shadow resume lists those big face-plants you have experienced and what skill or lesson you gained as a result (remember Arianna?). Invariably, our clients realize that their best skills and their "go-to" strengths were skills they learned through some kind of disastrous failure.

The first advanced course in psychology I took as an undergraduate was called "The Psychology of Human Learning." I failed. Being the bright kid that I was, I figured that if I couldn't pass a course on learning, perhaps I did not know how to learn. That summer I took the textbook with me to my job as a camp counselor, and I studied everything I could find about how to get stuff into my head in a way that I could retrieve it. I have aced nearly every class since that summer. I didn't get smarter; I just learned how to learn and study. To this day I use many of those skills with my clients. Take a moment and create your own "shadow resume" now and see what comes up for you. Go ahead and take the time. We'll wait.

The third law of motion applies especially when you decide to change or transform yourself. The moment you make that declaration, the world around you will push back with an equal amount of force. The bigger your declaration of change is, the greater the pushback will be. A little change will be met with a little pushback. Maybe your family that is used to your being a certain way will react negatively to your new attitude and behavior.

But suppose you are up to something big. You desire to manifest your highest purpose, your personal vision of excellence. Depending on how strongly your declaration is made, you will be met (almost immediately) with a powerful "challenge" from the universe. Seemingly, everything that looks like it will stop you will be in your face. It's like deciding to go on that diet and the next day you get invited to three parties! Making a declaration will cause you to see the forces working at odds with your stated intention.

It is almost as if the universe aligns itself to challenge you by defying you to make your stand happen. Universe says, "Oh yeah, if you're serious about that, handle this!!" When you venture into the world of possibility and transformation, you begin to expect that equal and opposite reaction as a measure of how strongly you have made your declaration. Later on, in this book we will discuss how we even view our breakdowns as a manifestation of the equal and opposite reaction. But for now, suffice it to say that the equal and opposite reaction will always be there; the equal and opposite reaction makes it look like you will never be able to do what you had declared or intended; and (perhaps most importantly) the equal and opposite reaction is a powerful indicator of the strength of your conviction.

These three laws are the most prominent and visible of the many laws of nature and the physical world with which we live in harmony. We cannot violate them and by the same token we are not punished if we try to stray from them. Though we cannot deny their existence nor violate their mandates, knowing what they are and how these forces act upon us gives us the ability to align with them and move into being the source of our experience. Knowing the laws that govern movement and growth, we accept their reality and progress from trying to fight them to aligning with and using them as part of our power.

Think of a time when you wanted to do something big. Perhaps it was a thing you attempted that everyone else thought was a foolish idea. But as soon as you had decided you wanted to do that, then some obstacle appeared in front of you. What was that big idea? What was the equal and opposite resistance that you encountered? What was the force that was acting on you and how strong was your intention that was "accelerating" you?

The Observer Effect

There is a curious phenomenon in physics (and in particular in a subdivision of physics called quantum mechanics) called the "observer effect." While the whole description is beyond the scope of this book, you can get a brief and quite understandable explanation of the whole phenomenon from Dr. Quantum.[4] But the bottom line of this observer effect is that the presence of an observer alters anything that the observer is watching. When scientists first studied and attempted to measure subatomic particles, they found something curious. If they were looking for weight, they found that the neutron or electron had mass, but it had no observable energy. However, when trying to measure its energy, they found that it had a charge but no mass. In other words, what they looked for they found, but finding that one attribute masked their ability to see any other.

The wildest of these studies was called the "double slit" experiment. In this case single particles of light (electrons) were shot at an object with two parallel slits. The assumption was that the particle would go through one slit or the other and project two corresponding bands of light on the wall behind it. But that wasn't what they found. Instead, they found that the two slits produced multiple bands of light on the wall behind, indicating that the single electrons were acting like waves not particles (something you can see if you drop two pebbles into a still pond—where the two rings of ripples overlap, it produces a multiple effect of patterns). That wasn't the weird part, though.

---

4 "Dr. Quantum – Double Slit Experiment," YouTube, Dec. 27, 2010, https://www.youtube.com/watch?v=Q1YqgPAtzho.

When the scientists placed a camera on the back side of the double slit wall (presumably to see if the electrons were doing something screwy when passing through either slit), the very process of having something observing the particles passing through the two slits produced only two bands of light on the wall. In repeated variations of this experiment the result consistently happened—no observer produced multiple wave bands and the presence of any type of "observation" would result in only two bands.

What does this have to do with you becoming the source? It is simply this: Your presence in this experiment called life alters that which you are capable of seeing. You will not only see just that which you expect to see, but you will be unable to see that which is not your expectation. Your presence in your life has a skewing effect on what you are able to see, perceive, and know. That means that you cannot trust your perceptions as providing you with complete data. There may well be far more things happening and swirling around you than "meets the eye." In the next section on psychological foundations, we will discuss how your mind further complicates this, but for now, let's just leave it as your role as the observer of your life alters that which you are able to see.

A Word about Time

Based on what he could observe of the physical world, Sir Isaac Newton surmised that time was a linear mathematical constant. He proposed that time was a fixed, observable principle that was experienced equally by all humans. In other words, we all get the same twenty-four hours, and that's that. Newton's thinking was so widely accepted that when someone came along and questioned it, that challenge made little impact on the thinking of the masses.

That someone was Albert Einstein. Einstein found in his research that time was not a constant, that in fact it is fluid and will "bend" when subjected to forces like speed and gravity. Time is relative and can be experienced by two individuals differently depending on what they are doing and where they are located. Einstein's theory of relativity, though widely accepted and even discussed in high school science books, is not something that most of us understand on a personally relevant level. Of course, we all have heard the applied story of relativity where one twin brother goes into space for an extended period of time traveling at or near the speed of light, while his brother stayed behind on good old planet Earth. Upon his return, we would see that our space brother had not aged but a few days while his Earth-bound twin was much older.

Why is this relevant to our conversation? How many times have you gotten so immersed in a project or a problem that when you looked up at the clock in what you assumed had been fifteen or twenty minutes and found that several hours had passed? Perhaps even most of a day, having completely missed lunch!

But isn't the opposite also true? Have you ever been so engrossed, so enthralled in what you and your friends or colleagues were doing, packing so much excitement and activity into the moment that you were certain that hours had passed and you'd better head on home, only to find that it had just been forty-five minutes?

How could both of those scenarios be true and a common phenomenon we all have experienced? The only way that these experiences could be true is that our sense of time, which Newton physically experienced as an exact measure of the passage of events in our lives, is in actuality fluid and relative. Einstein called this principle space-time and theorized (then proved) that the space-time continuum is elastic and both situational and non-situational. In other words, things that might normally take time to travel from one situation to another could actually happen in the same time irrespective of place (recall the split atom experiment referenced earlier in this chapter).

So let's apply this to our work of being source. Everything you need or could want in life is present right here and now. Because space-time is fluid, all possibilities do, in fact, exist now and require no time for cooking or thinking up or waiting for the right moment to appear. They are all here, now, in the present. The problem is not in their existence or "real"-ization but in our ability to see past our Newtonian rigidity into the reality and fullness of the present moment. For now, we will hold on to that as true and work with it as we move forward.

Finally, your capacity to see the abundance of things you need and see them manifested in present tense real time is directly related to your ability to be in the present, fully present to the moment. The more detached from the present you are (either distracted by the past or the future or your own thoughts and emotions), the longer it takes for those benefits to manifest. Said another way, once you get these concepts of the physical universe, the ability to access them is dependent on your ability to be and stay present.

Change is Constant

While on the topic of universal laws, another relevant to personal development is that the nature of life, the universe and everything (to borrow from Douglas Adams, the renowned author of *The Hitchhiker's Guide to the Galaxy*) is change. As we said, the one constant is that nothing is constant and nothing lasts forever. Unfortunately, the major function of the human brain is to make order out of this continually changing and chaotic world. Our minds create words, classification systems, boxes, buildings, and roads (and so much more) in order for us to better cope with the chaos and change. It is only natural then that our minds do not like change much, if at all.

But if we recognize that change is and will always be with us, then we should get some tools and methods for living within change. Taking a fifty-thousand-foot view of things, we can see that evolution is nature's way of dealing with change. As the pressures of new environments squeeze in on living things, they either evolve or they die and become extinct. The mechanisms of our physical bodies are a result of that evolutionary process. We didn't just arrive here. It would be presumptuous of us to think that evolution has come to an end with the form of things as they are today. Evolution will continue.

On a micro-level of our own lives, the same will also be true. While we may not perceive the evolution happening, it is certainly going on. We were born in the middle of the 20th century and, in our lifetime, we have seen technological advances that have either morphed our minds' functioning or altered our habits. Just a tick ago (on the cosmic clock) people would memorize and recite extensive texts like the *Bhagavad Gita,* a five-thousand-page tome of mythical stories. The portion of our brains that would have that capacity may still be present, but ask any twenty-year-old to memorize and recite a five-page document, or even the Declaration of Independence, and you will often meet resistance.

The point of this discussion is that we are always evolving, and we evolve, in particular, *because* of the *tough* changes. Breakdown of our systems, our own coping mechanisms, and our bodily defenses force us to adapt and evolve. That is not something you have any choice in, as a matter of fact and a matter of nature. However, what you do have a choice on is how you intend to react to change. If you start with the assumption that change is the constant, then you can anticipate that things will most likely change and that what you set out on as your path will have some twists and turns. Furthermore, if we assume that changes will occur, that life will invariably throw us a curveball, then you can be prepared to shift gears and directions as needed.

Adaptability to change is a skill that you can acquire. But it is nothing more than being prepared to drop your agenda and shift—to roll with the punches—and reset your intention. Be aware that just because you have an intention and you have made an unalterable commitment for your goal, the world will not roll over and play dead. It is more likely the case that the universe will show up in a way that will test your resolve. But let us be clear here. It is not white-knuckled pressure to get what you declared that is the key factor. It is your ability to recognize the change and adapt to it, evolve because of it, and move forward on a different tact, that will prove to be your success. Not every change is tough enough to cause an evolution or transformation of you, but some will come along that will certainly put you to the test.

Presence

One final concept within the realm of our physical world and time is that of presence or being present. We often talk about presence as a state of being or as a noun. But the real truth about presence is that it can never be "attained" as a state, because now does not actually exist. Think of it: there is a nanosecond before Now and there is the nanosecond just after the Now, but the actual moment of Now cannot even occupy the space between those nanoseconds, no matter how thinly you slice them. That is because time (or the measurement of time as we often think of it) itself is fluid. Time flows. Einstein proved that spacetime actually bends around different energies—thus time is not even linear.

So when we speak of being present, we are in pursuit of an elusive or nonexistent "now." One might consider that to be a meditative or contemplative practice–focusing on your attempt to occupy now. A similar exercise might be this one: If you meditate with a singing bowl, one practice is to get the bowl singing and then listen for the "last sound" as it trails off into the inaudible nothingness of not emitting sound. In much the same way, focusing your attention on finding now can be a practice of quieting the mind through extreme attentiveness.

Being present becomes an active state of awareness to the billions of things and insights and awarenesses that are available in the space between before and after. As with studies in physics, we suddenly find this smallest space opening up to infinite awareness—awareness of the incomprehensible infinity of all things that live in the moment. We spend much of our days and our lives so bombarded with the loud, large things of daily living that we often fail to see all else that is also present alongside those bright shiny objects.

Though now never actually exists as a definable moment, its pursuit is worthy of your best efforts and can produce a level of awareness beyond imagination. Many sages teach about becoming present or about experiencing the now, usually through meditation and contemplative practices. But some Central and South American tribes have medicine rituals designed to help the student experience now through the use of hallucinogenic herbs. Carlos Castaneda's recounting of the teachings of the Yaqui shaman, Don Juan, details the use of jimsonweed and peyote to produce a deeper awareness of time. In South America, Peruvian shamans use a combination of combination of Ayahuasca vine and other herbs to create a dream-like state that permits the user to seemingly slow time to a standstill to experience "now."

But before you go trekking off to the jungle, try experiencing now as best you can on your own through meditation. Take the next few moments of not-yet-now, or of just having missed now as it passed, to intensify your awareness of what actually is. One simple way is to use a bell or a singing bowl. Give it a ring and then still your mind as you listen to hear the last sound of the ringing bowl as it trails off into nothingness.

Owning Your World

You are not separate from this world. In truth you are inextricably tied to and woven into the fabric of the universe. While you may feel that, compared to the universe, you are an insignificant speck of dust, you are as much a part of the fabric of the universe as the sun or the most powerful black hole. In essence, every bit of the universe is reflected in your being.

The French scientist Benoit Mandelbrot coined a term for this called fractal. Fractals are self-repeating patterns that happen on massive scales in the universe and can be seen in simple expressions all around us. On the universal level, you can see the spiral arms of most galaxies, but what we don't see is that same spiral shape in galactic clusters and, it is theorized, in the universe (or what we now believe are multiverses). Closer to home, a simple example of a fractal is a cauliflower. Notice how the shape of the entire cauliflower is also the same shape of one cluster and that, if you take just one floret or bud off and look closely, the top looks just like the entire cauliflower. Mandelbrot found that these self-repeating patterns are the nature of all things. We see it in our DNA and in the capacity of stem cells to create or recreate any differentiated organ. We are part of the whole of the universe and that it is reflected in us just as we are reflective of its pattern. You and I are just florets in a big head of cauliflower of humanity. In fact, science has found that 99.9 percent of our DNA is exactly the same as every other human. It is only that 0.1 percent that accounts for skin color, gender, eyes, and all the things we see as our diverse differences.

Then, if we are so closely tied to each other and to the world around us, we can begin to see our part in the world. But we want to take that one step further. You are not simply a passive part of the world, but an active force within it. Your movements and even your thoughts are forces that set things in motion within the world (and universe) around you. We just got through a section that said that an object will either stay at rest or stay in motion until it is acted on by an opposing force. Now we are saying that you—your being, your thoughts, your actions, and your intentions—are a force that cause not only other things to move, but are the source of those equal and opposite reactions as well.

What this translates to is that everything you see around you, everything you have experienced, and everything that is provided to you by the "outside world" is in part caused (sourced) by you. Or more simply put, you own your world. You caused this experience you are living in. You were part of how it came into being and the trajectories of your past experienced life have brought you to here. Own it! What we mean by owning it is that you actually see what part of it is yours—how you got here, what these other players are doing, what you know, what options you see or don't see, your resources and so on. In many ways and for the most part, these are all of your making. As our friend Michael Strasner says in his book on *Mastering Leadership*,[5] "When you believe someone else is keeping you down or preventing something from happening in your life, you've given up your power and are in a victim conversation, which will produce the results and experiences consistent with being a victim."

Naturally, when we contend things like you own your world, someone will ask the hypothetical (or real) question, "What about a victim of rape or molestation? Are you saying that they caused it?" No, of course not. But denying that event's link to their current situation robs them of any potential for interacting with it in a way that moves them forward or upward. Certainly, too, we all have experienced rough times in our past that we would feel we didn't cause—that we were in fact victimized. True. But again, failing to recognize our part in the dynamic that occurred totally disempowers us and leaves us no alternative than to be blindsided again by some similar situation. You may not have power over the actual event that occurred to you, but you are responsible for your interpretation and the equal and opposite reactions caused thereafter.

This is something that I can speak personally to. When I was five years old, I was sexually molested by a family member. Obviously no five-year-old is responsible for an event like that. But what I want to add is that I do take responsibility for the thirty years that followed that. For many years afterwards, I used that abuse as an excuse for feeling like a victim to men, for a life of promiscuity and for living with a low self-esteem. Then, in my mid-thirties, at the point when I had come to grips with owning my power and was ready to get married, I reached out to my family member and forgave him. I told him that I was finally living a full and happy life. I no longer wanted to hold that over either one of us. Doing that did not take away the fact that he did this, nor does it really change the fact that I had been victimized. Rather, it was finally taking ownership of my life.

---

5 Michael Strasner, *Mastering Leadership: Shift the Drift and Change the World* (New York: Direct Impact Publishing, 2018).

Thus, when we talk about our ownership of our world, we are advocating a position that sees our role in everything around us. It is a position of power and effectiveness without which we are simply ineffectual blobs, floating through a chaotic world and subject only to what the outside world wills for us. We would be perpetually victimized by such a position. But the truth we understand is that you cannot live in two realities at once. Either you resign yourself to being the victim or to owning the world you live in. You can't be half and half. It either "is what it is" or it isn't. Why wouldn't you want to take the position of ownership?

As a practical example of owning your world, imagine that you have a commitment to sprucing up the environment and eliminating waste and litter. You often take it upon yourself to pick up any little scrap of paper you encounter and toss it in the nearest bin. But owning your world goes much further than that. It means that when you encounter that random bit of litter you start questioning yourself about how strongly you are holding your commitment that it would be even possible for others around you to have littered. Are you saying enough? Are you publishing your tips for others and the values and benefits others could reap with a cleaner environment? Are you taking every opportunity to communicate the importance of a clean environment to others? Because, you reason, if you are owning the whole thing, taking full accountability for the results that show up around you, that litter would likely not be there.

I am a deeply spiritual person and have an advanced degree from a seminary. I assure you that it is neither blasphemous nor anti-religious to contend that we each are partners in cocreating our world. We will not be using theological terms throughout this book, though we certainly could. The problem is that religion, belief systems and spirituality are profoundly individual and personal choices. Each of us has our own belief system— whether theistic or atheistic. The marvelous thing about believing in an Almighty "one" is that within that is the capacity to show up in whatever form each of us needs. If you need a god who performs miracles and walks on water, that is how it appears to you. If you need one that is the underlying ground of existence or simply the causal force behind everything, that too is how it shows up for you. And of course, if you have no religious belief structure, that is how it appears to you as well. So we use the term Universe (capitalized to signify its authority) to represent that which is far greater than we are.

We are not playing God in thinking you control the universe. You are not delusional about your powers or your personal importance, whatsoever. This is not about God/YHWH/the one, or any deity. When you are standing as source, you simply see everything as results and feedback on your stands and commitment. Of course, this is an odd example that doesn't fit the paradigm. But the point is that when you own your world, you own everything that shows up in it and can no longer turn a blind eye to what is there. It is either there because of your actions or because of your inactions, and is a result of the fact that you are in your current environment. You are the source of those results. We will go into much greater detail of what it means to stand as source later in this book, but for now, owning your world is an element of your interconnectedness with the entirety of creation. You are as much a part of it as it is a part of you.

Here's a way to put being source for it all into practice:
One of the practices that my husband and I use when I feel not respected, taken for granted or even like a victim is the following exercise. Think of a time when you felt misunderstood, undervalued, disrespected, or otherwise in a "less-than" position. It may be with your boss or a lover or a friend. Write a letter from that person's perspective (not yours) explaining how that other person must be feeling. And if you really want to add power to the process, take time to sit with that person and read your letter from them to you. Not only will you be amazed by the results, you will often see how their feelings parallel or match yours!

Laniakea

Laniakea is a Hawaiian term meaning "immense heavens" or "wide open skies." It refers to the sense of awe and wonder you feel when looking at an unblocked view of the night sky. Looking up and seeing the bright band of the outer arm of our own galaxy, the Milky Way, and noticing the brightness of other relatively close by galaxies and visible stars, you can't help but feel incredibly small and infinitely large at the same time—small in comparison to the many billions of stars and universes out there, and yet immense as you feel that you are a part of this incomprehensibly large system. You are both insignificant in the grand scheme of things and yet an integral part of that whole. Without you the universe is incomplete. Without you, a star is missing from the galaxy of which you are an important part.

If you have ever done this in the wilderness, on a mountain top, or in the desert, you know what Laniakea really means. Distance means nothing, looking up at the sky. The illusions of feeling like you are floating among the stars feels dizzying. You get perhaps a sense of being overwhelmed and a feeling of being at home among the stars. That feeling is a sensual element of standing as source. You are a star; you are cosmic and you are eternal. And you are finite, temporal and small at the same time. That is the reality of the physical world. When you look out into space and recognize the immense distance between those stars, you are also aware of the gravitational force they exert on each other. You can get the same understanding looking into an electron microscope and realizing that most of what we think of as solid is actually composed of empty space between variously charged particles.

Laniakea calls us to make a choice: Are we going to see the greatness and the immenseness of our being and take our place among the stars and physical forces of the universe? Or are we going to feel small and insignificant, playing little in our insignificant tiny world? The choice is yours, as it always was, and always will be. What's it going to be: Standing as source, as a force in the universe, or hiding in the shadows and playing small?

Kris Girrell & Candace Sjogren

Section Two

Psychological Foundations
of Source

Kris Girrell & Candace Sjogren

–2–

Perception Is Not Reality

In nearly every liberal arts college offering psychology as a major, you can find an advanced course labeled something like "Sensation and Perception." This course studies how the brain reads information sent to it from the five senses and how these data are recognized and converted into thoughts, sensations, images, sounds, and memories. To make the point that it is the brain that sees and hears and then interprets the information it receives, the instructor will often show a video of a famous video experiment[6] wherein a student is given a pair of glasses fitted with a prism in front of each eye, functionally inverting the image that is sent to the brain. Through the inverting prism glasses the world looks upside down. At first the student has difficulty knowing up and down, but then she successfully pours milk into a tea cup. After a day, the student walks about quite a bit more easily but still at times reaches up for something that is low down. However, by the third day she is riding a bicycle and functioning normally.

The experimenter at that point has the student remove the inverting glasses and she almost freaks out because, without the glasses on, her brain

---

6 "Inverted Vision Experiment Clip," R.C. Hartman, YouTube, July 25, 2013, https://www.youtube.com/watch?v=MHMvEMy7B9k.

is now seeing everything upside down! Yet, in only a matter of a few minutes the brain readjusts the image and she can see normally once again. To the astonished participant's mind, the message is clear: The brain did all of that changing and adapting. The brain knows what is up and down and what gravity and heat cause things to do (water pours down and flames rise up). So, it eventually reorients the information it is getting to fit what normal should be—what it knows to be true.

For those of you who believe, here is another example of the power of the brain. If you wear glasses or lenses, you know that the two eyes are often not equal in their visual strength. What normally happens is the fuzzier image of the one eye will be matched into the clear image of the other eye to provide a clear, binocular (3D) image. Often contact lens wearers who need bifocal lenses will be given one lens corrected for reading close images and another for seeing at distance. Anyone who has done this can tell you that the three-dimensional, binocular image they see is clear, and that they do not notice the fuzzy image as part of the picture. The brain does all the work by creating clear perception out of two different images. This is how powerful the brain is.

So, what does that mean for the purpose of our discussion? Simply this: Seeing is not "out there" as some objective reality. Two of us can stand on the same street corner and witness an accident. We can touch the same bent fenders and still, as long as we do not discuss it, we will file different accident reports. Your mind makes sense out of the things you perceive and that sense-making process is inside your brain. That means *what you see and what you perceive as a reality may not in fact be what I see because our brains are loaded with different events, education, socialization, and vocabularies.* And it is that stuff inside the brain that makes sense out of the data that comes in through our eyes and ears. Let's dig into this a bit more.

In Malcolm Gladwell's book, *Blink*, he talks about "thin slicing." Thin slicing is noticing that we have an initial judgment in the first split second of each encounter, judgments that are based on our biases which we call our unconscious biases. The issue is that we come to trust our unconscious biases as the truth in our perceptions. Gladwell has a particularly informative exercise which we suggest you try right now.

Write down five or six words you associate with dark (perhaps dark colors or things like nighttime, alleyways, and shadows.). Then write down five or six words you associate with light (sunshine, colors, or windows). Duplicate the list so that you have two lists of the dark words and two lists of the light words. Then time yourself on the following:

Beside each of the dark words in the first list, write a *G* for good or a *B* for bad. Do the same thing for the light list – *G* for good and *B* for bad. Note the time it took. Go back to the second two lists and place a *G* beside all of the dark words and then a *B* beside all of the light words. When Gladwell timed people on this process it typically took twice as long to do the second part of the exercise, demonstrating that as powerful as our logical minds are, we still are operating with biases that affect our processing and our understanding of the world of events around us.

What you see and hear is filtered and interpreted inside your brain. But, wait, there's more!

You Never Get the Full Story Anyway

It is one thing to note that the information we perceive is filtered, altered, and made sense of by our brains, and another to note that when that information is communicated by another person, we will not likely get the full picture. What others tell us about what happened has already been filtered once by their brains, as they perceived it. Then that message gets altered again as they attempt to find the "right" words to describe what they saw, heard, or experienced. This is even further reduced when we live in a social structure where the hard and less appealing information is not spoken (like in some families and in many work environments). We simply don't like giving what we think is bad news or negative feedback.

Many leaders don't receive the full story, partly because those informing them want to tell only about the successes in an effort to look good or fear their boss won't want to hear the negative information or learn that something is not working. In one company we know of, scientists were working on a new drug that seemed on the surface to have great potential. The researchers discovered however that part of the compound that goes to the brain is not eliminated. It builds up and has the potential to become toxic—a fact that the senior leadership did not want to hear. As a result, the compound got all the way to clinical trials in humans before the FDA shut it down. The company lost millions and was eventually bought by a competitor.

Take a good look around you. Are you surrounded by a family that doesn't like disruption or negativity? Did you grow up in a family that would avoid conflict in the name of family harmony? What about your friends? Do you have the type of good friend that will tell you when you have a piece of broccoli stuck in your teeth or you have bad breath or your zipper is open? Or do you have really "nice" friends who tell you you're great and they have your back? We have the kind of relationship where we actually look forward to soliciting feedback on each other's experience of what we do. We have the depth of a relationship that is based on love and mutual respect. For example, when one of us says to the other person that our experience was of them waiting to say the next thought while the first was speaking (as opposed to listening), that feedback is designed to build the depth and quality of our relationship so that it gets stronger.

Friends will be friends and coworkers and employees are well intentioned. You just will be getting filtered information—either because of their selective mindset or because of the filtering their mind does when choosing the words to say. Both the input filtering and the output filtering are what we call context. Contextualizing information is filtering it through the sense-making process, either when receiving input or when selecting our words as output.

But not seeing or hearing the full story goes a lot further than just the feedback you do or don't get from your friends and associates. What you see in the world is only a thin slice of reality as it fully exists. You can't know everything for two reasons. One is that you have only two eyes and two ears and one brain and are therefore only one seven-billionth of the human experience, which we would have to conclude is quite tiny! But, two, the nature of the universe is chaotic and unpredictable. As much as our minds would like to create some semblance of order out of that chaos, it has very little capacity to overrule chaos itself.

One example of not knowing or being able to control chaos comes from my honeymoon. Andrew and I were taking a trek in Nepal not long after the great earthquake in 2015. Our guide was Kumar, a man who lived west of Kathmandu and in the epicenter of the quake. Kumar's entire village had been destroyed. But Kumar was a man of his word, and he had contracted with us as a guide, so he took us up-country for our adventure. Kumar told me that the government had given each family a sheet of metal which they had folded to make a makeshift metal teepee for temporary protection. He smiled as he said it was all right, except when it rained, because then the snakes would also seek shelter under the metal roof.

While we were out, Kumar got word that the Nepalese government had decided to give each family six hundred dollars with which to rebuild their houses (believe it or not, that was enough to build a small house in Nepal at the time). All of the men of the village were taking a bus to Kathmandu to get their money, but Kumar could not because our location was nowhere near the village. On the way to Kathmandu the bus swerved off the narrow mountain dirt road and all the men of the village—except Kumar—were tragically killed. When Kumar returned to the village, he was the only adult male. What really impressed Andrew and me was how he simply stepped in to help all the other families rebuild. He had not considered himself unfortunate that he could not go with the other men, nor fortunate that he was not killed in the accident. He just accepted that life was unpredictable like that.

Deconstructing Your Beliefs

When we are confronted with this evidence that what we see is filtered and tainted by our belief system, we suddenly are faced with the task of trying to deconstruct our beliefs. Where do they come from and how do we unearth them? We suggest starting from a place of acceptance: That the very best we get will be to realize that no matter how much we work on deconstructing our belief system, we will always have one. We refer to this as your default context, but for now, let's address having a context that is made up of our collected lessons, education, life experiences, socialization, and heritage. These lessons are the pool in which we swim as children and eventually become the ocean in which we swim as adults. We are steeped in it so completely that we are often not even aware that it exists.

Having a lived experience simply means that our mental memories are shaped by what we have learned when things happen (when we experience them). Our lived experience is not right or wrong, per se, but we get to decide as adults whether those interpretations serve us. As children, things just seem to happen to us and with help from our parents, teachers and friends, we "put them into context." Perhaps a fire truck blew past you as a little child and the siren frightened you. Parents calm you down and tell you about first responders and heroes and one of those bricks was put in place. You were told not to stand outside or go swimming during a thunderstorm, and another was put in place. These are easily seen.

But what is far less visible is how we form beliefs about who we are, what our ethnicity means, what it means to be male or female. Our parents didn't tell us what to think if that information does not line up with what our actual experience is, if it is not one of those binary choices that our parents were afforded. Somewhere we learn to identify our tribe or group and identify who is not in our tribe.

Depending on where you grew up, you may have been taught that those who look different, or whose religion is not your tribe's, are to be feared or held as suspect. You may have learned that your future is yours for the taking, that you are entitled to "get ahead" and become "someone," even president, if you so desire. But you may have grown up in a pool that told you repeatedly that you were nothing and would amount to nothing. You may have been taught either explicitly or surreptitiously that your skin color, gender, or sexual orientation makes you a target.

All of these—literally everything that you think or from which you react—has been learned. And faced with the prospect that some or most of those learned beliefs no longer serve you and the values that you are living, we get to figure out how to *deconstruct* them. This may not be easy, both because it is so difficult to separate out what is the source of our behaviors, and because they are so deeply ingrained in our mind.

Systemic Racism

Allow us to take this on by addressing a very large elephant in the room: systemic racism in our world and in the United States. America was founded on a precept of religious freedom and human equality—at least those were the spoken words. But in truth, our nation was founded during a time when slavery was a widely held belief, often substantiated by the misinterpretation and misuse of Biblical passages (also written in times when slavery was popular). Slaves were considered as not human or subhuman and as a result when our founders penned the line "all men [sic] are created equal" that did not include the rights of slaves (or women for that matter). Woven into the fabric of our society as a new world was the age-old principle that certain people, specifically in this country, those of darker skin color, were not entitled to the type of respect that was afforded the White ruling class. It was not written in our founding documents; it was not articulated in our churches; it simply was the understanding that was implicit in everything we did.

Our society has matured over the last 250 years and we would like to believe that as a more mature society, those racist views no longer exist. But it is terrifically clear, even as we are writing these words, that the unspoken beliefs of racial inequality are still operating quite powerfully and, in fact, have become built into our systems of government, law enforcement and "justice." Skin color is seen as a symbol of criminal propensity. African-American men are incarcerated at more than five times the rate of whites, and African-American women at double the rate of white women, according to the NAACP (National Association for the Advancement of Colored People). But those figures do not include Hispanics and other nonwhite groups. Research shows that a nonwhite "sounding" name on a resume is less likely to be selected by recruiters and HR professionals than one with a more traditionally white sounding name—despite having identical resumes. And, conversely, changing the name to "whiten" its sound more than doubled the likelihood of being called in for an interview.[7]

During the writing of this chapter, in the first week of June 2020, our nation watched, with horror, a viral recording of a police officer holding George Floyd on the ground by pressing his knee on George's neck, while bystanders pleaded with him and the other officers to stop. George was lying on the ground face down with his hands tied behind his back. He was not resisting nor fighting and repeatedly said, "I can't breathe," until he lost consciousness and died. While the gravity of this explicit killing swept through the country, it was not an isolated event. We have read so many examples of how deeply flawed our law enforcement system is that we have

---

7 Dina Gerdeman, "Minorities Who 'Whiten' Resumes Get More Interviews," Harvard Business School, May 17, 2017, https://hbswk.hbs.edu/item/minorities-who-whiten-job-resumes-get-more-interviews.

almost become immune to their occurrence, until one so clear and evident catches our attention.

We bring this up not in an attempt to sensationalize the event but to take on the difficulty of dismantling deeply rooted misbeliefs. Irrespective of where you stand on the issues of racism and irrespective of the color of your skin, we all must face the fact that systemic racism exists and shapes our country's behavior. So rather than just taking on the hypothetical belief that you or I might hold, we will use the clear reality of a systemic injustice based on racial beliefs as our example. How we do it is the issue here.

The first step in changing a belief is to recognize that it exists and is having an adverse effect in our lives. Whatever your position in life, we all own the responsibility of learning what is happening and the length and breadth of its current effect. We must recognize it and name it in no uncertain terms. It is called racism. It does no service for us (nor for anyone, actually) to claim that we are not racist when we live in a racist society. If we are not recognizing the impact it is having on a daily basis, we are in denial of its reality and have no ability to deconstruct it. And by the way if you, the reader, are Black, Indigenous, brown or even a white-passing person of color, you already know this truth and have seen more examples that you would ever care to.

Secondly, we are to find where it is impacting our lives most. How is racism (in this case) impacting the functioning of the society? How is racism affecting you? What are you not able to understand and learn because the books you read, the classes you took in high school and college were written from a skewed perspective? Do you want to know the truth? Does it cause you pain that you have been sold a package of lies about our history, about our legal system, about your neighbors, and about the atrocities committed against the people native to this country? Take inventory of the real costs of racism on your life—and please fight the urge to say "none." One way many of us have done this is by reading and journaling along with the book *Me and White Supremacy*,[8] which we highly recommend.

The third step in deconstructing our beliefs is to identify what the replacement belief is for you. Throughout this book we will be talking

---

8 Layla F. Saad, *Me and White Supremacy: Combat Racism, Change the World, and Become a Good Ancestor* (Naperville, IL: Sourcebooks, 2020).

about your vision and your values. "Visions and values are responsibility, integrity, authenticity," says our friend and trainer, Michael Strasner in his book *Mastering Leadership*. No doubt your vision is one that includes such ideals as peace, harmony, love and acceptance—the exact opposites of what we see when witnessing a murder such as George Floyd's. What this step equates to is changing the headlines we read in the news. It means changing the concept of a White woman calling 911 on a Black man in Central Park in New York City and falsely reporting that he was threatening her (an actual event the same week as the George Floyd murder). That might read as "woman *accepting* a Black man for reminding her to keep her dog on a leash"—or *loving* him and *expressing gratitude*. If that sounds silly, then start inspecting your own beliefs more deeply. What are the headlines you have and how might you change the story they feed your mind?

Which brings us to the fourth step in deconstructing our beliefs: dialogue. When we were children, we went through a phase (at about eighteen months) where we were fearful of new and strange people called stranger anxiety. But we should have outgrown that many years ago. If we are still uncomfortable with the presence of things and people we don't understand, it is time to begin learning more about them. Ask questions and learn about who those "other" people are. Why do they do what they do? Who are they as individuals? Or just shut up and listen! Understanding is the key to dismantling beliefs that skew our actions, whether our reaction is one of racism or fear of the unknown. What builds a system is the wholesale acceptance of conditions or beliefs without questioning them. It is only through the hard work of dialogue and outreach that we can begin to dismantle a system of mistaken and misinformed beliefs.

The fifth step is to begin changing the actions (ours and those of others around us) each time we catch it happening. When people are uncomfortable and project their discomfort on to others because of the perception they have of that other person, that action is racist (though we could say sexist or classist, xenophobic, or homophobic as well). When we change the action, we alter the interpretation and story about the situation and begin to alter the system. But the very thought of calling an emergency number (911) because you are uncomfortable with a situation in itself is a ludicrous action and furthers the amplification of the racist discomfort. It sets in action a response of sending armed personnel to resolve a situation that might easily be resolved by other means and other social services.

All five of these steps form a foundation for committed action. We each must work to alter the existing narrative that permits covert and systemic racism to exist. This final step in deconstructing our beliefs is to take repeated actions consistent with the values we espouse as part of our vision. When we continually act in this new way, we habituate the desired belief of equality, humanity, compassion, acceptance, or whatever we hope to be living as our values.

Deconstructing Your Beliefs

Try the following exercise to apply these steps for deconstructing your beliefs:

1. Notice where you are not seeing the whole picture when someone points out that there might be another way of seeing things. Write down two or three beliefs that might be operating instead. Give that belief a name (for example: "Money doesn't grow on trees"). Call it out as a whole system of related beliefs (for example around finances or career potentials or marital relationships).

2. Expand your list by noticing where else this (these) belief(s) has (have) an impact on your life. In what other arenas might you be impacted by this set of beliefs?

3. For each belief or sub-belief, write out an alternative that counters the logic or thought in the belief. For example, you may have a set of beliefs about financial scarcity (as in, you don't have a lot of money and don't see a way to make more). One subset belief might be "Money doesn't grow on trees!" That being the case, your replacement might be "Money is flowing everywhere."

4. Start by listening to others and the beliefs that they hold. Listen to people that are good with money and know how to manage it well. Ask what they do and how you could apply it in your life. But the key is to really listen. Don't listen to see where they are wrong (your belief will want you to do that). Listen with what the masters call

"Beginner's mind."

5. Identify the action that you will take that is consistent with the new belief. If your new belief is "Money is flowing everywhere," then perhaps you need to be part of the flow by giving a gift of money to someone more needy than you are. How much will you give and how often will you give it?

6. Do it! Practice it and live it as your reality. Until you have done it enough times to produce a mental "muscle memory," you have the possibility of slipping back to the old belief. Keep practicing.

"To truly communicate your vision masterfully, you must bring your intention alive in the listener. You must bring it alive in such a way that the listener is so connected and empowered by the vision, the message, or the possibilities you're communicating, that they take hold of it as if it is their own." (Strasner, *Mastering Leadership, 2018*).

COVID-19

Another event that unfolded during the writing of this book that also points to the power of interpretation is the coronavirus called COVID-19. Unlike its two previous relatives SARS and MERS, the COVID-19 strain of coronavirus was much faster acting and had far worse effects on its victims. Also unlike the previous ones, elderly people seemed more susceptible than youth and children as was the case with both MERS and SARS.

Partly because it was a flu-like virus, and partly because both MERS and SARS before it were able to be handled, many people and many governments did not recognize the severity of COVID-19 until it reached epidemic proportions. That is where the interpretations began. The interesting factors of interpretation that emerged pointed to both individual interpretation and cultural differences. For example, some countries reacted swiftly and rigidly to the tactics of isolating and preventing the spread of the virus, by virtue of their cultural style (an example might be Israel or South Korea), while others took the approach of believing in natural immunity (Sweden) or highly resisting the policies and procedures because the people felt they were a threat to their individual freedom (USA).

Locally, we all experienced the inconvenience of the lockdown. Some of our friends worked at companies like Oracle and Microsoft that simply transitioned to virtual working for all employees. They believed that they were working harder than ever because of the innumerable Zoom, Teams, and Webex meetings they had to attend. Others who were small business owners had to furlough or outright lay off their workers because of the shutdown. And both of us actually lost all business and contracts for the following three-quarters of the year because of the ramifications of the virus. Some people lost money on the markets; some lost their jobs completely. The effects were as many and as varied as there were people experiencing them.

But the interesting thing to us, while writing this book, was how each person reacted and interpreted the impact on them. Some were depressed and devastated by the loss of work and a paycheck (despite getting some enhanced unemployment). One friend talked about how stressful it was on him and his family. Others got out their resumes and started looking for what they could do next. And some, unfortunately, were immobilized by the grief and pain of lost loved ones.

Throughout the COVID-19 crisis, while both of us lost friends to the disease, and an entire book of business as a consultant and trainer totally vaporized, both of us remained excited about what the future—a very unknown and unpredictable future—held for us as possibilities. Since nothing like this had ever occurred before in history, we both found ourselves thinking that it was a blank canvas on which we could paint whatever we wanted. The bottom line for us was our interpretation of this event as an opportunity made so many exciting things possible.

—3—

Circumstances Are Not
What You Think

For most of us, circumstances are our "current reality." "It is what it is." But if we are *source*, we are going to define current reality as a particular set of circumstances. We chose to call them circumstances because of the word itself. Literally it is derived from two roots: *circum*, a preface from Latin that means around or surrounding, and *stare*, for standing as in a place or being. So, circumstances are the things that stand around you. And because they are standing there, we think both that they are real and that they should be contended with.

But it is also true that what you see is a product of what your mind thinks is there and not necessarily what is there. What you see as your present circumstance and set of conditions in which you are living and operating are more a product of what you are able to see (or comprehend) based on your vocabulary, experience, education, and socialization. The brain can alter the data it receives to make a clear or more logical image, but for now let's just say that:

- You do not see with your eyes or hear with your ears (those are just the receptors of stimuli which are decoded and understood in the brain)

- Because your brain learns and makes sense out of those stimuli through a process called "associative learning" (this is like that), it tries always to interpret the conditions and circumstances through what it currently "knows."

Therefore, when you are in a novel or unique setting, your mind is rapidly trying to match it to previous experiences that you knew how to handle or had experienced. And given that this is a unique and novel setting, the mind will morph it into what it knows already (not the other way around). It does the same thing with new circumstances, challenging circumstances, and even hostile situations.

Because of this power our brains possess, we come to understand that though we "see" our current reality somewhat accurately, our brain is shapeshifting that information into what we understand. And what we understand is not the present or future; it is 100 percent made up of our past experiences. Learning occurs when we take what we already know and use it in novel new ways to create a new concept.

Anthropologists tell us that the Carib natives of the islands now known as the Greater and Lesser Antilles were fierce fighters and cannibals. They were a male-dominated and warring society where only the men spoke the language and women conversed in another tongue (called Arawak). The main culture of the Carib was traveling to other islands in dugout canoes to raid and conquer them. They tortured, killed, and ate the men and captured the women as slaves. All in all, the Carib were pretty tough customers.

But when the Spanish came to the islands, the Carib stood passively, dumbfounded, while the Spanish soldiers made a sport of decapitating them because they had no reference for "canoes with clouds on them" (ships with sails) and people with shiny metal heads and chests. Those images made no comprehensible sense whatsoever and they were dumbfounded until it was too late. Irrespective of the Spaniard's superior weaponry, the Carib did not fight or even resist. Such is the power, which may sometimes be to our detriment, of the human brain.

The net result is that what you perceive as your current circumstances may not be exactly as they are, and worse yet, may not even be there at all. We understand our surroundings through the collective understanding of all those around us—despite the fact that they (as did the Carib) may have the same limited experiences we have. In the chapter on physical foundations, we discussed the observer effect. If you add the observer effect into this equation of the mind being able to only see what it has the ability to describe or match to previously learned concepts, you begin to understand why things aren't as they seem. You can begin to understand why we contend that there is more "out there" than we think or believe. And if the combination of the observer effect and our internal perceptions is what is really happening and causing us to see only the limited set of choices in front of us, then why not operate from a supposition that what you need and desire is actually present and available despite not being able to "see" it?

Our perceptions are further muddled by our beliefs and understanding. We may believe that a certain situation is irresolvable. We may believe that there is no way out. We may believe that we do not have the mental or physical or emotional capacity to deal effectively with a situation. Those beliefs are also a result of our education, socialization and experience. We may have grown up in abject poverty without any financial means to achieve our hopes or dreams. So, when challenged with a large financial obstacle, we may believe it to be impossible, not because it is an insurmountable amount of money, but because our experience includes no history or information on how to achieve that. When we are faced with a roadblock in our career, we may have no understanding of how to shift gears or skill sets to move forward and we are either passed over for the promotion or flushed out of the system completely.

The critical skill is to begin by separating the event or circumstance from the meaning your mind is placing on it. The former part requires building a skill in observing and getting input from other sources as to what the condition or situation actually is. All we see is what we think we see, and will swear on a stack of holy books that what we heard was what was actually said by some other person. We need to begin by checking our understanding at the door and trying to get a better grasp on what the actual situation is. That is the easy part, believe it or not.

A friend says to you "I'm not coming to dinner." You may have an immediate interpretation, such as "They are blowing me off." In the first step, we challenge you to seek out additional information. What is happening in your friend's life that made coming to dinner impossible? It likely had nothing to do with you.

The second part is even harder. The next step is to question all of your beliefs about how things are or the way they are and become suspicious of your own beliefs. Like in the example above, you may have the belief that "People always blow me off." Things, people, and events have no inherent meaning in and of themselves. We give events and things meaning by applying the defining skills of our brains. Even 911, on its face, has no meaning by itself. It is a collective event where a few men commandeered and flew a few planes into a couple of buildings whereby several thousand people died. But what you and I interpret those actions to mean is what makes it an important or even a life-defining event. Our fathers and grandfathers enlisted in the military the day after December 7, 1941 because it was for them "a day that shall live in infamy." But when we read about Pearl Harbor in our history texts, I would wager that you barely had a twinge of emotionality. It was just an historical event.

There is an old Zen tale about a farmer who had only one horse for tilling his field. One day the horse ran off, and his neighbors came over to console him, saying, "That is so sad and awful. It is too bad your horse has run away." But the farmer responded, "Maybe yes, maybe no." The next day the horse returned with three mares following him. Again, the neighbors said, "What great fortune it is that you now have four horses." The farmer remained unmoved and just said, "Maybe yes, maybe no."

When his son was then trying to tame the wild mares that day, one tossed him off and he broke his leg. "How awful—what bad luck," the neighbors cried. And of course, the farmer just shrugged, "Maybe yes, maybe no." The very next day the emperor's troops came through the village drafting all the young men into the army. But the farmer's son was not taken because of his broken leg. Again, the villagers praised the farmer's good fortune, but of course the farmer just smiled, "Maybe yes, maybe no!"

Meaning-making happens in your head. And such is the case for all of your so-called circumstances. They may not be as you see them or think they are. But we want to be clear about what we are saying. There are two realities: 1) what actually happens as an event or situation, and 2) what you interpret that to be through your meaning-making. External events absolutely still occur. A pandemic swept the globe in 2020, catching many of us unprepared. Those external circumstances are real. It's just that how they appear to us is so powerful and strong an interpretation that we will never fully know what the reality was. We will only know our interpretation of it, the meaning we placed on it and our relationship with that meaning. Pearl Harbor happened. It's just that it occurred as a significant and meaningful set of circumstances to our parents or grandparents while that same event had no power over us today.

The bottom line with circumstances is that what you think is an urgent issue, a limiting roadblock, an oppressive set of dynamics, or simply an impossibility is mostly an interpretation of what you see dimly through your own eyes. What you would swear you heard even when you can repeat the words back to the other person does not have the same meaning as what the speaker intended. That being the case, you can choose to interpret those words, events, and situations differently, not as a flight from reality, but as your stand as a transforming person.

Susan is a brilliant woman and respected professional. While most people call her powerful, they also quickly add stubborn and opinionated as a modifier. She is the daughter of an engineer and three of her four siblings are also engineers. Growing up, she ran everything she was taught or experienced through the litmus test of logic. If it was not logical, could not be observed, or could not stand up to the test, it was not permitted or was dismissed outright. Thus, when Susan considered a career, the projected possibilities of success (or more like statistical probabilities) were all that she considered. She was highly driven to accomplish and had rather lofty goals, but they were always calculated.

As a result, Susan led a somewhat conservative life, never being outrageous, never risking what she might perceive as a failure by not achieving what she had set out to do. As she put it, "When I make a commitment, I guarantee you that I will deliver, and I have never not completed that to which I have committed." She often would add that her dad had taught her that her word was golden and the only thing by which she would be measured.

Then, one day, Susan was in a personal empowerment training course with about 125 other people. The trainer had posed a simple question for which Susan was certain there was only one answer/solution—hers. But in the ensuing discussion, she heard close to 125 other and different ideas of how that situation was interpreted and could be solved. These were smart and accomplished people, but they did not see things as she did. How could so many people be so wrong and so blind as to not see her solution? It suddenly hit Susan that the situation was not the issue but rather how it impacted each person differently. She described the feeling of "a thousand dominoes" falling over in her head. She was suddenly aware that hers was only one interpretation and that there were possibly hundreds or thousands of other interpretations and began questioning all of her previous assumptions about her world. Right behind that thought, she recognized that she had never risked for any great goal in her life. She always chose the sure route and the route that could be seen clearly from her point of view. That moment, she says, changed her life.

Circumstances Are Always Changing

Circumstances are momentary and continually changing. Your limiting belief that the current set of circumstances is fixed, solid, and immutable is just another belief that stands in your way of interpreting your situation and coming up with a solution. Listen to your internal conversation when checking into your thoughts about the situation you are in. Key words you might notice are "always," "never," or a certain "is-ness" (as in, "that is just the way it is."). All of those thoughts place your circumstance in fixed and permanent mode and render an interpretation that it will never change and that you will not be able to do anything about.

But circumstances do change. Constantly. Moment by moment. One of the great truths taught by the masters and sages of every era and of every discipline is that change is the only constant. Nothing lasts forever, not our plans, not our finest moments, and especially not our circumstances. In fact, nothing lasts for very long at all. Even a concrete wall cracks and crumbles over time. Not even our own personal walls can protect us from change and from our changing circumstances.

The only solution to dealing with change is to become aware of our interpretations—and that we have interpretations available to us—of the current changing circumstances, and then become willing to alter those interpretations, and alter them again and again as they continually change in front of us. In order to master this process, we need to look at our actions and reactions as a kind of trial-and-error system to test the effectiveness of our movement and reinterpretation. Keep asking yourself, does this interpretation further my progress?

Exercise:
Get a three-by-five note card and write out your best five questions to help shape and refine your interpretations. Below is a starter list but don't feel you are limited to these—make your own that best work for you.

- What is the blessing in this current situation?
- What am I learning about myself and other people from this?
- Does this help me understand what the real situation is?
- What feedback can I get if I try a different set of assumptions?
- What will move me forward toward my goal?
- What is the next "best" thing to do?

Often, we feel stuck when circumstances change and feel out of control. A second exercise in dealing with changes is what we call the "Options Workout." Identify a situation in which you feel totally stuck or for which you see only one option (and not a good one at that!). Then list five other options you might pursue. Let's say you feel stuck at work and you are doing so poorly with it that you feel the only option you have is to quit. You then brainstorm five different options. You might consider: 1) Approaching your boss and asking for help, 2) asking a more successful colleague what they suggest, 3) asking for a transition to a different job within the company, 4) taking a leave of absence to refresh your perspective, or 5) perhaps taking a quick training program to learn a related skill.

Next, review your five options with a loved one and ask for their input. What might they add or delete from your list? Get guidance from them and talk over the prioritization of your options.

Finally, bring whomever will be affected by your decision into the conversation, but in doing so, allow them to have options as to what they can do with the information. Schedule time to talk out your difficulty with (using the work example above) your boss (the person most closely related to your difficult situation). But here is the precise formula to follow:

1. **Schedule** a time to talk stating that you want to discuss something very important.

2. Before saying what you have decided, tell the other person what **your concern** is about it. For example, you might say to your boss, "I want to talk about something very difficult, but I'm afraid that you may think less of me, or that I might lose your friendship —or worse yet that you might fire me.

3. Follow that immediately with what you **hope** for the other person's reaction to be. "But I hope you see me as a friend and colleague, care about my well-being, wish me well and support me in this decision."

4. Then **state what your decision or action is**. "So after much thought about my performance, I have decided to leave the company."

5. This allows for the other person to react and perhaps to make alternative suggestions for solving the problem.

Everything Is Feedback

Once we begin to see that the situation around us will provide information on our perceptions and interpretations, everything becomes feedback. Feedback is defined simply as a return of information about a result or process. However, a word of caution is that your understanding of the feedback, itself, is an interpretation that has been filtered through your existing belief system, and you will need to be skeptical of your own interpretation of the feedback. It is critical that you have that healthy skepticism in place first before using your understanding of the feedback as a course correcting source, lest you fall victim to your own self-fulfilling prophetic beliefs. In addition, be wary of your evaluation of the feedback ("I like it or don't like it" or "this is bad news or good news"). Feedback is just information.

For instance, if I were to lose my job, it would be a source of feedback on how I may have been showing up as an employee. But if my context is that of being a victim, my interpretation would be to begin looking at the situation to see what was wrong with the company, my manager, and so on. The feedback would not "land" in the manner in which it intended. Rather I will begin collecting evidence with the feedback to support my point of view. Unless we begin with an understanding that reality is illusive and that we are only perceiving our interpretation of realities, we have little chance of allowing the feedback we receive to help us shift.

What does that mean? First of all, the physical world stays balanced through a system of action and reaction, or as we noted in the third law of motion, through action and the equal and opposite reaction. Therefore, whatever you do (or for that matter, whatever you think) is an action to which the universe around you will react. This reaction is what we refer to as feedback. Often we think that feedback is when someone "unloads" their opinion on us. But in this text, we mean the naturally occurring set of reactions to what we just did, said or thought.

But understanding that means that we first admit that we do not actually see the whole picture. Our perceptions are tainted both by what we thought we did or intended to do and by what we think we are seeing as a reaction. To further complicate this picture, if that reaction or feedback loop is coming from other people, we also understand that they are reacting to their perception of what they *think* we said or did. Learning to be skeptical of our perceptions helps us to become more curious about what those reactions (which we are choosing to call feedback) really are. Later on in this book, we will delve more deeply into the whole aspect of feedback and the use of feedback when we are standing in the position of sourcing our lives. But for now we ask you to recognize that much of what we see as our current "circumstances" are actually reactions to what we have done or how we have been showing up in the world and with our friends and loved ones. It is all just feedback.

You Are Not Your Past

When you are asked to describe yourself, you probably do what most of us do and describe your history of experiences, roles, and accomplishments. Those are the things through which we build a self-concept. As a child, perhaps you were a fast runner, or maybe you were the last kid picked. Whichever was the case, your mind made up a story about the meaning of those things. You identified as a certain gender (or perhaps as none). You were good at math and sciences or maybe hated writing. The list goes on. These experiences eventually built up into an icon of who you see as yourself. It is how you know yourself. But that is not who you are—not in the least. Most of what we think is our past are not the events of our lives but the memories we have about them.

A friend of ours (we'll call her Rachel) was physically and sexually abused by an adult neighbor as a thirteen-year-old girl. It was a horrible and degrading set of experiences that no one should ever have to experience and she has our deepest compassion for having survived. Worst yet, it lasted for more than a year. But the problem that was associated with that was that she felt that she had become worthless, that *she* was trash and just something to be used by others. As the result of this horrible event, her teenage mind made up an explanation of how and why that could have happened. Strangely, as is often the case, her first thoughts were not of the villain, the perpetrator, but of her value. She concluded that in order for anyone to treat another person like trash, that person must be trash-like. She just internalized the feelings and made the whole thing about her lack of worth. It probably didn't help much that her mother didn't believe her and called her a whore when she finally did talk about it.

Though quite attractive as an adult woman, Rachel never dated men she was attracted to and often felt that she wasn't really liked by any of her boyfriends. She dropped out of college and married the last of her many college boyfriends because she was pregnant. Now, with four grown children leaving home to pursue their own careers, she is beaten and depressed. It was not until someone she respected (her coach) got her to see how beautiful she was as a person and how he marveled at the loving way she parented her children and treated others around her that she began to think that perhaps she was not damaged goods. But digging out from under a strongly held self-concept is a long process.

No matter what happened in your past, even the most horrible of abuses or conditions of poverty, your memory of those events and how you interpreted those events *are not the events*. What happened to Rachel was deplorable, but what she learned as a result of trying to figure it all out was a story that shaped her life for the next thirty or forty years. *Your past cannot be changed but the story can.* That does not mean that you become suddenly happy about the past and make up a fairy tale about some awful event in the past was good. Rather, it means that you can question, inspect, and reinterpret those events from the perspective of the adult you have become. Because you were the last kid picked as a nine-year-old does not mean you are a loser. It may have been that your body did not mature as quickly as the others and they just wanted the bigger or stronger kids first—kids like to win! It meant nothing about you. Their choice was based on their desires and thoughts about winning. Because your dad took a belt to your backside every time he was in a foul mood did not mean that you deserved to be abused. It means your father, though trying to cope as best he could, was abusive. And no child deserves to be abused. But you are not a child today, and the decisions you make today are your own, not your father's, and certainly not the story and interpretation of the five-year-old version of you.

Your past is a set of events that occurred (or at least you thought they occurred) a certain way, but your story most often will not be a mature evaluation and interpretation of those events. This same distinction is true for current events as well. You may be in a relationship that turned sour gradually over the past months or years. And lately it feels like it is dragging you down. In moments like this, it is important to distinguish between what is happening and what you are interpreting about what is happening. They are two separate things. It's like saying rainy days are downers, as we said before. Because it is gloomy outside doesn't mean you have to be gloomy. Likewise, a destructive or dysfunctional relationship does not have to mean you are dysfunctional. Later we will address how we can be the source of some of those less desirable things and events in our lives (and what you can do about that), but for now, we just want to underscore the idea that your story about a situation is different from the situation itself, whether that is in the past or happening right now. Stories can take on a life of their own and when we find ourselves reacting to the story instead of dealing with the reality it can have undesired results.

When I was four, my family lived in the army housing on a base near Stuttgart, Germany. The kids of those families had no real playgrounds and often ended up playing on the sidewalks and steps outside the long, four-story apartment buildings. As I recall those days, I had always had this vivid memory of a terrible day. I was playing with some toy about which I was quite possessive. The other kids started taunting and teasing me calling him names like "stingy" and such. Frustrated and angered by their teasing, I looked around where I was on the stoop. On either side of the three steps leading down to the sidewalk was a low curb made of bricks and half of one of those bricks was loose and not connected to the mortar around it. In my rage, I vividly recall picking up the brick and throwing it at one of the kids. It hit him on the side of the head and he immediately began bleeding profusely. I got so scared that I ran in and hid under the table in the kitchen. It was as vivid a memory as an adult as it was when it "happened."

Some forty years later I was in a personal empowerment seminar when the trainer started challenging our personal beliefs and self-concepts. One of mine was not just that I was big and strong but that I was capable of violence. "I could hurt people if I were not careful." Asked when I first had that idea, my mind suddenly remembered the event back in Stuttgart. But I was encouraged to be skeptical of the story, challenge my memories, and do some research.

That evening I called my sister (the lord and protector of her little brother back in Germany), and asked her about the event (she would have been six at the time and perhaps could recall it). She told me that she had remembered the kids teasing me and she recalled a time when I hid from them under the table for some reason, but she had no recollection of the brick. So I called my mom with the same question. What she said absolutely floored me. She said that all the moms in the barracks were always in conversation with each other, all the time. If anything like that would have happened, not only would she have known about it, all the moms would know it and would have been talking about it for weeks. "No," was her answer, "That could never have happened."

What did happen was a scared and upset four-year-old boy had so much rage inside himself that he wanted to throw a brick and saw that happening as a thought or fantasy, and that thought had lodged in my mind as fact and hardened into a construct for the next four decades. I neither threw the brick (nor could have the athleticism to throw it and hit a target) nor had I injured the other boy. I only *wanted to* and *thought* about it. All of my life I had been so certain that it was a fact. The memory of the event was so vivid. *And yet, it never happened.*

We wager that the two of us are not the only ones who have ever done such a thing.

We urge you to begin questioning the interpretations you have about yourself. Of course, we mean only the negative and self-deprecating stories. Please don't discard such beliefs as "I am a beloved child of the Divine" or other strong and empowering beliefs! But some of that old, smelly stuff in your brain needs to be challenged and overturned. You will not believe how freeing that can be.

Changing Your History Story

Here is a fun exercise to repackage your history, your interpretations of your historical events that have become the story you perpetuate.

1. With a group of trusted friends (it takes at least five other people to do this exercise) have each person write down the three most life-defining events you've experienced— good, bad or ugly, it doesn't matter.

2. Pair up and in front of the first person tell that person what happened in each event (try to be brief by keeping to a two-minute time limit).

3. Switch to a new partner and tell all three events as though they were the worst things that could have ever happened to anyone—even if the event was positive!

4. Switch again and this time tell the story as though you were a reporter on the evening news. Give the facts almost with a monotone and dispassionate matter-of-factness.

5. Switch to a new partner and tell the same three events like Pollyanna would. "My mom locked me in the closet, but it was really nice because I learned how to read in the dark and I felt so cozy there."

6. Switch to the final partner and tell the three events in a language that has never been spoken on the Planet Earth before. But make certain that you are in fact telling the stories—just in gobbledygook.

7. When everyone has completed, have each person tell about their events but notice how the events have become just a story. They no longer live as "life-changing" events—they are just stories.

Our life-defining events are not about the event but rather the interpretations we have added to the events. But like my brick story, they take on a powerful role in defining us throughout our lives. But we learn in this process that it is our interpretation story that has all the impact. This storytelling process is sometimes used in treating PTSD for combat veterans. They are asked to tell the horrifying event(s) to their group. Then they are asked to tell it again and again, over and over, until it has become a story to them, and has lost its immense emotional charge.

When you reach the point where the story can be told without it having an impact on you and your emotions (and it will, with enough practice), you are ready to lay the story down and move on to writing your next chapter.

How Emotions Are Created – The Mind Is a Curious Thing

Feelings seem to arise out of the moment or happen without any forethought. But current research in brain science is finding that not to be the case. Lisa Feldman Barrett, a researcher at Northeastern University in Boston, is finding evidence that emotions are actually manufactured by the brain.[9] Barrett says that monitoring the brain in situations that produce emotive responses shows that what happens is the brain perceives the situation, rapidly surveys its memories for anything similar to that and then immediately projects the associated memories onto the future (whether that

---

9 Lisa Feldman Barrett, *How Emotions Are Made: The Secret Life of the Brain.* (New York: Houghton Mifflin Harcourt, 2017).

be the next moment or then next year). All of this happens at light speed so that what it seems like is happening is that the situation produces the emotion.

So, for example, let's say you are walking in the woods and see a large bear coming your direction. Your immediate reaction is fear and fight or flight—or at least that is what it seems like. But Barrett says it's more like our brain perceives the bear, finds stored memories of bears being large carnivorous animals with sharp claws, projects that potential fate on our current situation and, desiring not to be the bear's next meal, produces a set of strong emotions and physical reactions that aid us in getting away as fast as possible. All in less than a nanosecond.

The real issue here is twofold: One is that the massive database of memories is so immeasurable, so much larger that our greatest supercomputer, that it defies anything we can imagine, and, two, it is constantly and continually in play—it never stops, and mostly (now that we are adults) it never stops seeking confirming data. So, let's return to our woman-friend who thought she was trash. Ever since her teens, she has seen situations through the lens of a broken person such that, as a fifty-something woman, she had massive amounts of evidence that she was cheap, trash, "less than" others and certainly not deserving of unconditional love. This despite having four kids and being married for nearly thirty years. The fortunate happy ending to the story is that she participated in a personal transformation program that resulted in her totally destroying her made-up story and seeing herself as a beautifully transformed butterfly.

Many of our reactions are habitual—how you respond when angry, what you feel you can do when hitting some impasse in life, and so forth. Here is a little exercise to add to your repertoire of responses, knowing that we only do what we have as our practiced responses. With a partner (spouse, lover, or best friend), perhaps as a date night, write out your typical reactions to anger, to frustration, and to perceived negativity from your partner (make three lists). Then together brainstorm a set of new responses—off the wall responses. Get imaginative and prompt each other to get way outside the box. You could scream in a pillow, do a wacky attitude dance, exercise, paint each other in different colors, smear ice cream all over each other's face—go for it. But the important part of the exercise is to pick a date/time and do them all—get the muscle memory in your head that you can and have done each of them. Then the next time a frustrating or angering issue arises, your brain will have a larger response repertoire and that can and will interrupt the pattern.

Another way to interrupt the pattern—and you need to set up the agreement to do this with each other—is that when one of you sees the other getting into that patterned anger (or emotional) reaction mode, shout "bananas" or look at your watch and say "it's 3:10 PM" (knowing full well that it is not!) or any totally non sequitur thought. The more radical and unrelated it is, the better it works. Doing something totally unexpected disrupts the patterned response. On the first interruption your partner will try to go back to the anger or frustration they were explaining, but interrupt it again. You will find that it only takes a couple of times before they cannot remember what they were trying to say or justify as their reason for being angry.

Breakthrough Means Breakdown First

It has often been said that as humans we will do far more to avoid pain than we will to maximize pleasure. We realize that most people think that they want to find joy, happiness, or pleasure, but in truth most of our efforts are in the opposite direction. One look at evolution, however, will quickly demonstrate that it is through pain, failure, and breakdown that we get better, stronger, and smarter. What is it that we learn in these painfully tough moments or experiences?

Let's first dissect what happens in a total breakdown. What do we actually mean by breakdown? It is important to differentiate that we are **not** discussing something like a "nervous breakdown." That is something that should be handled by a medical professional, and neither this book nor this specific chapter are intended to solve these kinds of problems. That being said, please read what follows through this important filter.

Breakdowns are, in fact, epic. Breakdowns are those places where everything we hold to be true in explaining our world and our current reality no longer fit or explain what is happening to us. You may feel like you have far more demands than can possibly be handled. Stress may have peaked at a level that you feel you cannot tolerate. You may be in danger of losing your job, your life partner, or your life savings. Breakdowns take all shapes and sizes—there is no exact formula, except that your breakdown will come in exactly the shape and image that you fear the most. And that is the first clue that it is a breakdown. (We will say more about fear, doubt, and insecurity in the next chapter.)

In the martial arts, we are told that there is only one opponent: ourselves. If we fear some competitor will be a great kicker or have faster hands, then one will appear who has those skills. But if we work toward stilling our inner fears, the opponent is just another person, just as skilled or not skilled as we are and just as vulnerable. Breakdowns are much the same. What we fear we cannot control will jump up and spin out of control. What we stress about will intensify or become far more complex to a level that our stress meter is pegged in the red zone. Our brains are these massive problem-solving computers, so as we begin to think of our worst nightmares and our fears, our minds happily get busy extrapolating on all facets of that problem set. Faster and faster it goes until it is spinning out of control with the myriad of consequences that will crop up if we do not handle this correctly.

Stress is quite simply being in a situation that demands more of us than we currently have the skills or tools to handle. In other words, we need to learn other skills than those on which we typically rely in order to handle this situation. But the big "aha!" inside that statement is that it is only *this* current situation that can push us to develop *that* skill or coping mechanism. Think about it: You can read all the books you wish about how to deal with an irate customer, but until you have someone directly in front of you, red-faced with rage, you will never really learn the skill of how to defuse that rage and solve the issue.

So the bottom line of breakdown is that it is the process of breaking down—deconstructing— some old habit or pattern in order to make way for a new one. Breakdowns happen in three phases:

1. There is some trigger event or thought that exposes the ineffectiveness, irrelevancy, or "pathology" of our own previous way of being or our previously held belief.

2. There is a period of confusion and disfunction where the old has been destroyed but the new way of being, believing, and acting has not yet been developed.

3.   There comes a point of reorienting into the new way of being that is often awkward or disconcerting simply because of its newness.

We often hear people say things like "I had a breakthrough on X last night," and while we don't want to rain on that parade, we think that many of those were more like epiphanies than actual breakthroughs. Breakthrough *always* means breakdown first.

On the back side of every breakdown is a new set of skills learned. Some of our best and most effective skills and values are gained not through practice, but through breakdowns. Generally speaking, we tend to think of our development of skills through what is called the "training effect." We want to get better at mathematics, so we take courses in math and practice using those concepts. If we want to learn to be good at public speaking, we go to Toastmasters and practice speaking in progressively longer speeches to larger and larger audiences. But the toughest leadership skills—like humility, compassion, and deep listening—are learned only by falling down in the game of life.

It is only through humiliation that we learn to be humble. It is only through crushing pain that we find compassion. And it is only in being blindsided that we finally open our eyes and ears enough to truly see and listen. That is the breakdown/breakthrough process. There are no shortcuts and there are no easy answers. Our friend and colleague Michael Strasner says, "How do you resolve a breakdown in a relationship when both of you are right? All it takes is one of you to throw in the towel, show humility, and acknowledge the breakdown, to apologize and be responsible." And as we always say, the only way out is through!

We all want washboard abs with only fifteen minutes of exercise a day. We all want transformation and to live a transforming life of abundance, but we often don't want the painful destruction of our comfortable belief systems to get there. Sorry. There will be tears, confusion, and uncertainty— sometimes short-lived as we experience in the container of transformational workshops, and sometimes insufferably long, like months and years. The length of time that a breakdown/ breakthrough process takes is determined by how attached you are to the old way of being (as in letting go). Once you get practiced in this way of learning, you will know that the real work is letting go of your attachments to how it is supposed to be.

"Wisdom comes from your experience of being in the process, from your ability to learn from any and all commitments in Your life on an ongoing basis. It has to do with contribution; it has to do with giving, it has to do with seeing possibility where one does not exist. It has to do with changing direction, changing course when the path you're on isn't working. It comes from owning your responsibility, owning your accountability. Wisdom comes from interrupting patterns and not repeating the past. Wisdom comes from changing behaviors and living the change." (Strasner, 2018)

Commitments, Considerations, and Circumstances

Into this stew of misinterpreted and changing circumstances we toss the next key ingredient: your commitment to be the best you that you can be. What you commit to is often a product of your understanding of the current set of circumstances. If you are a bit like Susan in the story above (only one way of seeing your world), you may rein in your commitments because you are so concerned about fulfilling each commitment and never falling short. But committing to something you have never attempted before or completed successfully won't necessarily produce success.

Generally speaking, we all understand what making a commitment to someone else looks like. We do it in the work situation all the time. We commit to a project deadline. We commit to some performance standard or quality assurance requirement. Even our employment contract itself is a statement of commitment. Outside of work we think of commitments we make in relationships—for example, as a marriage commitment. But most often people tend to think of a commitment as a sort of promise.

We suggest an alternative definition. When we are the source of our lives and our results, making a commitment involves two key principles: Commitments are unconditional and commitments alter your relationship with the rest of your world.

First of all, making a commitment is, above all else, ***unconditional***, or without conditions. It is not "I will do this if you do that." Commitments are ours to make and hold. When you place conditions on your commitments, you have functionally left the "back door" open. If you have made a commitment to complete a project within some specified time frame, and that commitment was contingent on another person doing their part, fulfilling your commitment might mean that you have to lean a little harder on the other person so that you can be complete on time. But it does not mean that you get to say, "Well, I did *my* part—it's someone else's fault it is not done." Owning the commitment means that you take full responsibility for its completion—not just your part.

It may also mean that you get to renegotiate the commitment parameters if it looks like you and your partners may not be completing on time, under budget, or within the agreements of the commitment. But this must be done at the earliest time possible. It doesn't bode well for anyone to attempt to renegotiate a commitment at the fifty-ninth minute of the eleventh hour. If you have a commitment to be somewhere at a certain time and notice as you get in the car that the GPS says it will take you an hour instead of the twenty minutes you had planned, the time to renegotiate is right then, as soon as you become aware of the possible broken agreement. Renegotiating your commitment is honoring the full intent of your commitment by finding a satisfactory new set of results that work for both parties. Using this definition of commitment forces a level of clarity into everything. When we make a commitment, we take stock of the conditions and circumstances around us. We make a commitment in full awareness that these conditions may change, and, despite those changes, we are committing.

The second element of a commitment is that it *alters your relationship with the circumstances around you.* The key word in that definition is the word relationship. When you make a commitment, how you relate to the other things in your life and circumstances is altered. When circumstances, conditions and things you have to take into consideration before you act are part of your awareness, then making a commitment takes on new power. No longer do the circumstances or your beliefs about them stop you. They no longer get to say what will happen. Your commitment becomes "senior" to your circumstances and outranks their power.

Consider the following two sentences, both of which have exactly the same words:

- "I want to go for a walk, but it is raining outside."
- "It is raining outside, but I want to go for a walk."

In which case will the speaker take a walk? In each case the dependent clause is the dominant factor. Rain is not an obstacle if and when you are determined to go for a walk. Likewise, your circumstances are less powerful than your commitment. It still may be raining, but that will not deter you. You may get a little wet, but taking a walk is more important. Your current circumstances and considerations are still there, but they no longer hold sway over your actions.

Combining this with the work you are doing on understanding how your beliefs and mental memories may have distorted your understanding of the current situation and your current capabilities, you may feel a new power and freedom in making commitments. Conversely, you may take more care in making your commitments so that they are based in a fuller awareness of what you are committing to. That is not to say that you are holding back, hedging your bets or playing small. Making commitments are bold statements while being fully aware of that to which you are committing.

One last thing about commitments is that we tend to "sell out" more on our commitments to ourselves that we will with others. Making commitments to ourselves is as iron-clad a promise as those made to others. In fact one of the most devastating things you can do to erode your self-esteem is breaking your commitments to yourself. Each time you make a commitment to yourself or others and keep it, you build credibility. Each time you break it, you lose credibility. Losing credibility with others concerns many. But losing credibility with yourself will cost you much more. Breaking a personal commitment is essentially saying that you don't matter. Keeping a commitment to yourself is something that can only be broken if you are not important enough to honor or important enough even to renegotiate with. Personal commitments are often the first to go. But once you start breaking your commitments to yourself, it opens the door to breaking other commitments—and the landslide begins.

Becoming source is a place of power, and that power begins and often ends with our commitments and intentions. Commitments and intentions are the bricks and mortar out of which we will build our powerful life and be able to live into that life as the sole source and author. Your commitments are now in charge, and you no longer have the option to break a commitment.

Intention – Adding to the Laws of Nature

Intention is not wanting. We often speak of having the intention to achieve some goal. But the confusion that surrounds that idea is generated by a couple of misconceptions we hold. We often think it is a matter of getting what we want. We say "I want more out of life," or "I want a better car, a better salary," and so on. But the problem with speaking into our wanting of something is that is not an intention to achieve that. It is actually a statement that affirms that we do not have that which we desire so much. Wanting is "lacking" by definition.

A second big misconception we hold is that most of us think in terms of the probability of our desire happening. It lives only as a hope against the odds. Intention is not hoping for something or about improving the probability of that something happening. Intention is a statement of certainty as if what we intend has already happened. It is for us a fact.

But the really insidious problem that undermines good intention is the ego itself. "The true definition of ego is the separate isolated self," to quote Michael Strasner again. Ego wants fulfillment for its own gratification. Ego is a hungry little monster that is never satisfied. It wants more and more because it thinks that these rewards are confirmations of its importance. And the problem is that while we all have an ego, ego has no place in intentional living. The ego and its drive for being separate from everything else and everyone else produces the suffering we experience as being alone, aloof, and cut off from others.

There is nothing wrong with having an ego. It is part of having a brain that can think about itself. And the ego is not necessarily bad. The ego is just a fabrication of the mind. And having an ego is important for the accomplishment of our goals. Ego tends to push us into achieving things. The problem occurs when the ego takes the driver's seat—when the needs of the ego are greater than the commitments that you make or stand as the main reason you are doing whatever, then ego is out of control. Despite having an ego, we all must be aware of our ego and of its demand for self-aggrandizement and need fulfillment. Our egos ought never be the reason behind why we are doing anything. Keeping our egos in check will not only serve us but others as well.

With ego in its rightful place—in service to our connection to all else—we have a shot at becoming intentional. Intentionality aligns our ego, our will, our energy, our spirit, our minds, and our bodies. Intentionality eliminates distractions and focuses our attention. We see more options, seize more opportunities, and we engage other people and other systems in moving with that intention. In short, intention alters our relationship with the outside world, with others and with our circumstances. In intentionality, there are no ifs ands or buts—there is only intention and direction.

Mike has ADHD and has a learned disdain of himself for always being late and missing his goals. As a result of doing that repeatedly day after day for fifty years, Mike is an angry man. He has innumerable derogatory nicknames for himself, the mildest of which might be, "I'm an idiot." But they go quickly downhill from there. Not only that, but they team up on him so that with each screwup comes a landslide of self-demeaning epithets that ultimately result in his self-loathing and anger. Mike asked to be coached in this process.

The first thing Mike had to recognize was that he actually had an intention. In fact, Mike had an extremely high intention of being perfect (which he defined as never missing a goal, never being late, and never making a mistake). Anytime Mike missed his intention, which was basically all the time with an intention that high, the "wolf," as he called it, would come after him and beat him to death.

We pointed out setting an intention was setting a direction and a yardstick with which to measure how close to the mark he got—not, as he does, to see how hard he needs to be beaten. We also pointed out that he would not even notice the screwup were it not for the fact that he does have such a high standard against which he was measuring himself. Perhaps others don't set the bar as high as he does, but having that high value is no reason to debase himself. Rather it is cause for recognition of having a great intention. How commendable!

Secondly, Mike learned how to be forgiving of himself. Robert Browning once said, "[one's] reach should exceed [one's] grasp or what's a Heaven for." He had to understand that falling short of such intentions is normal. We all do it. The difference is that others don't beat themselves up for missing; they simply see the act of falling short as feedback and keep looking at how to get closer next time.

Mike likes playing darts at the bar. I asked him what he did if he was aiming for a bull's eye and missed. Does he get drunk or beat himself up? "No," he said, "I keep throwing another dart to see if I can modify my release or arm movement so I can get closer." So, his intention to get a bull's eye and missing just showed him whether he needed to be higher, and more right or left. Intention is like that, and forgiveness allows you to pick up another dart. "Why not apply that to other things like being late or missing a deadline?" I asked. And he just started laughing, as though a great weight had been lifted off his shoulders.

–4–

Defenses and Defenselessness

Your Armor *Is* the Problem

For the most part ego defenses are normal and natural. They are, in a sense, a coping mechanism of the ego for its own protection and maintenance. But when we become ruled by our ego's defenses, our interactions with others and with the world around us becomes convoluted and even dysfunctional. Our defenses become a sort of armor that, while designed to protect, end up getting in the way of genuine and authentic interactions. Let's look at the most common ego defenses, why we develop them and how we might remedy them.

Below are the ten most common ego defense systems:

1. **Avoidance**. One of the most common defense mechanisms is avoidance—the act of steering clear of that which is undesirable. Our minds have created a story that certain situations are painful or potentially harmful and have found that avoiding them altogether is a good way to stay safe. Avoidance is similar to denial (see below) and serves to prevent us from having to deal with either the current issues facing us or the consequences associated with them.

2. **Compartmentalizing**. This common mental practice is a way of separating your life into independent sectors. For the most part this is a healthy practice like having proper boundaries. Compartmentalizing helps us, like avoidance, to focus on one task without being distracted by some potentially emotional other situation. An example of compartmentalizing is not talking about personal issues at work—generally accepted as a good practice. It allows you to focus on work issues while shelving your home concerns and worries.

3. **Denial**. One of the most common defenses (perhaps THE most commonly used) is denial. It is simply defined as the process of refusing to accept the current reality as it is. We have a friend who insists that he never lies and that lying is horrible. Yet he frequently leaves out important facts in relating an issue or swears he has nothing to do with something he was totally responsible for. Like our friend, you may block these facts out of your mind in order to avoid dealing with the emotional aspects of the situation or you may deny their existence because you may have to face some undesirable consequences that could result from them (as in Avoidance). Where denial differs from avoidance however is that denial is a total dismissal or negation of the situation and consequences, where avoidance recognizes the situation but steers well clear of them.

4. **Displacement/Projection**. In this situation you have a strong feeling but instead of allowing yourself to experience the feeling you either project that on to the other person (they are the bad guys) or direct it at some other person who is perceived as less threatening. For example, you may dislike people who have some kind of an accent, but instead of admitting that to yourself, you make up a story that they have an inherent hostility toward you. Displacing the emotions might look like getting angry about your partner's dirty laundry as opposed to confronting the issue of communication or relationship that needs to be addressed. Both serve to get you out of the "bad guy" role and make it about someone or something else.

5. **Intellectualizing**. This is a form of emotional protection by simply removing the emotional elements of the situation and trying to apply logic and intellect as a way of dealing with it. Instead of dealing with the emotion and allowing it to drive action, you may spend your time analyzing the various alternatives in great detail—almost building a spreadsheet of analytical minutia.

6. **Rationalization**. When confronted by a tough situation, you may feel a tendency to create your own set of facts so as to make you more comfortable with it. For example, if you were to get in a heated argument with a coworker that might require your making amends or dealing with the consequences, rationalizing would be making a case in your mind of all the things the other person had done in the past (not associated with this current event) that could be counted as reasons you were justified in unloading on that individual. These are your favorite excuses for your defensive behaviors.

7. **Reaction Formation**. People who use this form of defense actually recognize their feelings but choose to react in the opposite way. For example, feeling negative might not be something you like about yourself, so you decide that in such situations, you will only react positively and bury the negative feelings out of sight. For example, in an argument with your spouse, you may grit your teeth, yet smile and tell them you love them, putting on a happy face.

8. **Regression**. Regression usually happens more with children, but in some cases adults that have not been challenged sufficiently during their developmental years may regress to a way of being reflective of younger years. They may pout or have a childish tantrum that is totally unbecoming of their age or maturity. It is important to distinguish this from appropriate emotional reactions such as crying.

9. **Repression**. Many times, our emotions and the thoughts associated with them (See the section on how emotions are made) can be quite upsetting and make us uncomfortable. So rather than facing them (or the fact that your mind is creating them out of this reflection/projection process) you may unconsciously choose to hide them

instead— hoping that if you ignore them, they might just go away. This can have some nasty consequences simply because the reality, the situation, and the emotions do not really go away. Emotions, as we have said, are great messengers and directional indicators. If we repress them, they will eventually need to be reckoned with. Over time, other similar repressed feelings will build up a reservoir of emotional need, sometimes called "stacking," and come tumbling out at the least opportune moment and with an intensity that is disproportionate with the current situation.

10. **Sublimation**. The last on our list of the big ten is often considered a positive coping mechanism as well. In a way sublimation is similar to displacement in that the person redirects or channels a strong emotion into an activity that is considered safe or appropriate. Many of our male friends often choose to redirect their frustration at work into physical activities like martial arts or sports. Others may choose music or art as their outlet, while still others, for example, find building something a great way to deal with sadness, pain, or rage.

The bottom line here is that defenses are normal and natural and often do not cause any harm or ill effect. You may identify some or many of these in your own life and not think of them as harmful or in the way. Our point is simply that defenses, like any habit, can cross over the line of effectiveness and get in the way of your authenticity (who you are when nobody is looking) and accountability. As our friend, Michael Strasner, says, "Authentic communication happens when the words that are coming out of one's mouth and their private internal, non-spoken words are the same."

Being source requires that we inspect all of these behavioral patterns for what we can learn from them and for how we can become more accountable in our interactions with others. But it is terrifically important to be aware that you cannot take away an ego-defense without replacing it with some positive and adaptive behavior.

What Are Your Defenses—An Inventory Exercise

On a sheet of paper or in your journal write down each of the above defense mechanisms. Then for each defense process, list the ways in which that shows up for you. For example, under *avoidance* list all of the undesirable, painful, or disquieting situations which you try to avoid. Where do you *compartmentalize* your life in the hopes of not creating cross-over effects or where do you pretend to be more polite and civil that you know yourself to be? Be honest in this exercise. Below are some prompting questions, but don't feel limited to just these:

- *Avoidance.* What undesirable, painful, or disquieting situations do you try to avoid? Are there people you steer clear of or places that make your skin crawl? What about those people or places do you want to avoid?

- *Compartmentalization.* What areas of your life do you prefer to keep separate and compartmentalized?

- *Denial.* Whose existence do you hope to deny? What situations do you shove out of your mind in an effort to not deal with them? What parts of or people in your history would you prefer to deny or at least don't want to accept?

- *Projection.* Who are those people who just push your buttons? What is it about them that represents the qualities you most dislike in yourself?

- *Intellectualizing.* Where do you go into analysis or, worse, where do you tend to go into analysis paralysis? What areas of life do you tend to overthink or procrastinate?

- *Rationalizing.* What are your "go-to" excuses and truisms? One clue would be all of those situations or people you think are "always" that way. What are the areas where you already know you are "like that" because that's just who you are?

- *Reaction Formation*. Where are those places that are so uncomfortable that you put on the opposite way of being? Do you try to smile at a funeral or find yourself giggling nervously in tense situations? Dig deep on this one; it is often more than first comes up.

- *Regression*. Where and in what situations do you pout and stomp your feet like a rebellious teen? Where do you go for victim mode and claim you are not at fault?

- *Repression*. In what situations do you numb out (that can include stuffing feelings by eating, smoking, drinking alcohol, or other ways of dulling the emotion you feel)? Are there feelings that you just would prefer not to feel?

- **Sublimation**. What are some of the more constructive reactions you have to being upset? Do you go mindless in playing music or building a deck on the house? But most important, what are the situations that these methods of sublimation are used to deflect?

Becoming source requires that we not only understand our emotional reactions and our ego defenses, but that we get to the root of their causes. To become the full author of your life and create an unprecedented, free, and fully powerful future it will be necessary to clean up much of your automatic reactions, including many of your defenses. Being source is really being free to choose how to act and react or respond to situations. As long as these standard defenses are in control, you are not.

Safety is Not Derived From Our Power Defenses

If the ego defenses are primarily patterns of self-protection, the hidden result they are designed for is safety—safety for the ego and its self-importance. When we recognize that the ego has a need to continually seek validation through others and through our accomplishments, we can see the way in which our ego defense system operates and inhibits or even precludes healthy interpersonal relationships. The needed safety the ego operates from is to protect its own self-concept which is constructed out of a sense of scarcity and a feeling of "less than" or "not enough."

Becoming source, however, is based on confidence in the abundance of the universe—both the entire universe and that of our own immediate surroundings. Removing the ego defenses (or at least those that are overboard) allows us to do two important things in our transforming state of source: First, it allows us the ability to see all situations and consequences as feedback and as good information with which we can deal effectively. Secondly, it affords us the capacity to take ownership of all of our results. When we face up to and own our results, we become far more powerful than when we are hiding behind our defenses. True safety is found in having the power to deal with life on life's terms.

As source, we get to deal with the realities that life throws our way— many of which we had not sourced, as the universe is random—but then as source, we are not confined to reaction mode. We get to choose each action. If the world goes into economic collapse, we did not source that and must contend with life in reality and what the economic realities are. Those are life's terms. We cannot pretend all is well when in fact there is a collapse. However, and this is a big however, we are not constrained or limited to a subset of responses and are able to choose what fits with our values and world view despite the external conditions. That is life on our terms. Both realities are true. Recognizing that we are the source of both our great accomplishments and those efforts that have failed or flopped, we can move into the action most appropriate for the situation at hand and stand a better chance of moving through and beyond the current state toward a more desirable state of our intention.

The bottom line here is that our ego's defense system cannot handle the pure truth of how we are being in the world and how that produces our current reality. But the inverse of that principle is taking ownership and accountability for our current state of affairs decreases the need for those defenses to protect us and our delicate ego. Accountability is the remedy.

Having a Clearing Conversation – A Tool

The Clearing Conversation framework is a tool to support teams and resolve challenging or difficult situations that often arise out of misunderstanding, miscommunication, and/or mixing up facts and emotions. This process allows for a way to navigate those tough issues.

Use this model when you want to be in a solid relationship with another person. An individual typically wants to be in a trusting relationship with his/her spouse, children, extended family, and with his/her business associates. We are typically not in ongoing relationships with others with whom we have infrequent, business, or non-personal-sharing encounters.

The framework is not specifically intended for issue resolution, although that may result.

Its primary use is so an unspoken issue between two people does not distract them.

The framework is used when one cannot be fully engaged mentally and emotionally in the relationship unless the issue is "cleared" with the person.

Anger, anxiety, resentment, embarrassment, or other emotions that block the development of trusting relationships between any two people on a team will cause a weakness on that team.

Conflict is a normal part of everyday living—learning to address it is a valuable life skill.

The framework takes practice, and using hypothetical examples is a productive way to learn the process. Practice allows you to implement this tool in real time when the occasion arises.

When issues exist . . .

In most cases, clearing conversations can be performed in private or in front of a team if the team is practiced in this process.

Opening

The person with the issue starts first with a request for the clearing:

"I'd like to have a clearing conversation. Is now a good time? (If not now, agree on a time.) And if this is an okay time (or later when the meeting is set, the person with the issue begins with:

"The specifics of the situation are regarding our interactions last week." Then spell out the recordable facts; not judgments. In other words, saying that the other person was being a jerk last Monday is a judgment. But saying something like the following calls out the behavior without accusing the other person: "When you cut me off in the meeting and then refused to answer my request afterward, it set up an uncomfortable impasse between us."

For another example, "We had a meeting scheduled for 4 p.m. and you were not on time and then were silent on the call."

Still speaking, the person with the issue, then says: "I made up a story that . . ." or "I made this mean . . ." (I think . . . , In my opinion . . . , My judgment is . . .)

For example, "The story I created about it was that the meeting was not important to you, you are not engaged, you don't care, and that you are not playing as a team member."

And to conclude the opening points, the person speaking identifies her/his feelings: "I feel . . ." (sad, angry, scared, ashamed, guilty, excited, numb, happy . . .)

Ownership

An important element of clearing is for the speaker to take full accountability of their part in the interpretation/misinterpretation. Identify your part: "My part in this is . . ." (Your role in creating or sustaining the issue.)

For example, "My part in this is to be open and non-judgmental and I feel that I was hasty in judging you."

Adding to that ownership, the speaker states the way of being or actions that can be counted on after the clearing: "Going forward what you can expect from me is . . . ."

. . . And asks for a reciprocal statement of accountability from the other person: "Going forward I request . . . " or "And I specifically ask . . . "

For example, "Going forward you can expect me to give you a heads-up in advance. I request that you use your voice and contribute into the space because you are valued." It is important to add, "Can you comply with my request?" when you have finished with your part.

The other person is then provided with an opportunity to reflect and respond to the situation:

"Let me see if I understand you . . . " (Reflect or paraphrase without interpretation. Goal: seek to truly understand without rebuttal.)

After reflecting, ask, "Is that accurate?" (If not, reflect again or ask, "Help me to understand what part I am missing.")

The responding person can add: "Is there more?" (This is a crucial question. Ask in a kind, genuine, curious, want-to-be-in-relationship voice.)

<u>Clearing</u>

At this point, it is important to ask for understanding. The responding person should ask: "Are you clear about this?" (If "yes," you're done!) If not, then they should say what can be counted on going forward: "What you can count on from me going forward is . . . (Or regarding your ask) I agree/do not agree to do this going forward." (If the responding person does not agree with the request, they should offer another solution.)

Last, the responding person concludes with their request: "And I specifically ask...."

Clearing A Broken Agreement

A broken agreement occurs any time an individual makes a commitment to another and then fails to perform in accordance with that commitment. These events may seem little or insignificant but can build up over time if not addressed.

When an agreement has been broken...

"I acknowledge my broken agreement of . . ." (identify what commitment was broken)

"What was in the gap for me was . . ." (explain what was more important than keeping the commitment)

"What you can expect from me going forward is . . ." (explain what shift you are committed to creating)

We recommend practicing both clearing conversations with at least one other person prior to proceeding in this book.

Fear, Doubt, and Insecurity

While it may be true that our ego defenses, under the guise of protecting us, prevent us from seeing and working with the reality of our current feedback, the greater hindrance to our development and transformation is the triad of fear, doubt, and insecurity. These three emotions often stop us dead in our tracks. So, let's take a moment to explore their source and how they function in our lives.

Fear

President Franklin Roosevelt said in his inaugural address, "The only thing we have to fear is fear itself; nameless unreasoning, unjustified terror." Fear is a common feeling that arises in the early years of our lives as our minds see situations that far outstrip our meager skills and tiny hands. Even the smallest precipice looks to the child's mind like a bottomless pit that surely will mean the end of life! Loud noises (like a fire truck's siren) without the context or understanding of what it is, where it is going and why it is so loud, is beyond alarming to a child, and these early experiences produce a startle reaction and evoke a sense of fear. We learn to fear the darkness (and along with it, the unknown). As children become aware that not all adults are mommy or daddy, they suddenly feel anxiety around other strangers. Fear has its roots deeply dug in before we reach the age of adventuring and experimenting. Unless we learn to challenge our fears and learn that they are just thoughts and feelings based (for the most part) in our childhood, we will grow more and more fear-based as we mature.

Doubt

Doubt has its roots in trust, or more accurately in a lack of trust. When you first meet a stranger, do you have a tendency to trust them or to be skeptical? Saying that we are doubtful of others is like admitting that we do not trust their goodness. We do not trust them to be their word or keep their promises to us. We doubt that the universe will provide for us—that is, we do not trust that there is enough out there to provide for what we perceive as our needs. Doubt and its sister distrust live in the world of scarcity and the biggest impact is when doubt and distrust turn inward. Self-doubt—

the inherent distrust that we are enough as we are—is the foundation of all doubt. Think of it: if you cannot trust yourself to be enough, if you doubt your ability or capacity for doing what is needed, then how could you possibly ever trust others who are just as human as you are?

Insecurity

The third of this killer trio is insecurity. Like its siblings, fear and doubt, insecurity is all about how flawed and inadequate we believe ourselves to be. And like the others, insecurity comes from an underlying distrust in the abundance of the universe. The ego takes stock of itself and having arrived at the conclusion that we are not enough, it projects that on to the entire universe: there just isn't enough out there to take care of all of us and certainly that means I will not get what I need. The ego always needs more to feed its beliefs because it has come from a "not enough" story.

All three of these are more easily understood when we look inside of developmental psychology—that is, how we develop mentally, emotionally and socially. Scientists tell us that we learn 90 percent of our vocabulary before the age of five. All of your advanced, polysyllabic concepts learned in high school, college, and adulthood account for less than 10 percent of your vocabulary. So therefore 90 percent of your concepts about the world were learned before the age of five (because words only exist to define and categorize and understand the world). But during that massively accelerated learning phase, we were little kids and we were surrounded by things and people that were faster, stronger, smarter, and bigger than we were. And the byproduct of that is that while learning about our world, we were also learning that we were not bigger, stronger, faster, or smarter. We learned that we were just a little kid, less than the big ones and certainly much less than our parents and their adult friends.

This sense of inferiority was quietly and subtly absorbed into our subconscious young minds and formed the basis for everything we did afterwards. Essentially, we learned one of two responses to that inferiority system: We either said sadly we were just a twerp, a kid, less than, not enough, or we set out on a lifelong quest to prove the world wrong. We created an "Oh yeah, I'll show you!" attitude. But whether we succumbed to the "I'm not enough" approach or set off to show the world that you were big/strong/

fast/smart, we were working in reaction to the underlying experience of our childhood when we were just kids. Fear, doubt, and insecurity are that deeply programmed into our mental structures that we all experience some level of their effect even as adults. But because they are so deeply seeded in our psyche, they are extremely difficult to dislodge. It often takes a transformative experience for us to finally realize that those ideas formed in our early years no longer fit our world, and, while helpful when we were growing up, no longer serve us in the least.

Resentment

Deep inside, under all of the defenses, festering in some smelly corner of our minds lay our resentments. Here is where the real work of transformation to being and becoming source begins. Bill Wilson, coauthor of the guidebook, *Alcoholics Anonymous*, says resentment "is the number one offender. It ruins more lives" than anything else. He even claims that anyone who has not dealt with and removed their resentments will never recover.

We can look at our resentments in terms of categories like resentments we have about people, about rules, and even resentments we have about institutions. Think of those classifications in terms of a divorced person: There are resentments about the ex-partner, about the laws and the court system and even resentments about the institution of marriage or the beliefs taught by their religious tradition (another institution). You may not be divorced, but you can see how these resentment categories fit your own life. Once again, this is the turf of the ego. Resentments are offenses observed by the ego caused by others, by having to bend to the rules and principles of our society, peer group, and company, and by having powers greater than ourselves (actually our egos) tell us what to do and how we behave.

The ego wants what it wants, on its terms and in its timeline. In this case, the ego is like a rebellious child inside our head, throwing a tantrum when it doesn't get its way. "Fine," says the ego, "I'm never playing with you again!" The problem, however, is that these resentments never get resolved. Where the child in real life quickly forgets the tiff, our ego packs the resentment away and holds on to it as a type of logic and justification for "being the way I am." We think we are this way because we had to defend ourselves against the "slings and arrows of outrageous fortune" as Shakespeare called it. So, we add a little defense wall here and a style adjustment there, and add an attitude or judgment elsewhere, and over time resentments have become the source of our being.

One of the biggest areas of resentment we may carry around is when someone has lied to us. Most of us feel that lying is deceitful and wrong, of course, but in the world where we stand as source, there is another perspective we get to consider. Do you realize that it takes two people for a lie to happen? There is the person who is speaking the lie and there is the person who is buying into the lie. In order for a lie to deceive us, we want to believe something about what is being said. And in order for that condition to exist, there has to be something incomplete in our lives that sets up the condition wherein we desperately want to believe is true.

Take for example, lying in a relationship. Perhaps your lover falsely reports that he is in love with you (for whatever reason). If we have been missing love or never really felt unconditional love in a relationship outside of our family, that could set up a desire to want to be loved. In fact, it could be a desire so deeply needed that we might be willing to believe anything that sounded like a promise of love. And when that person leaves abruptly or cheats on the relationship, we feel we have been lied to and betrayed. While certainly we are not condoning the practice of lying, we get to own our part in the scheme. Were we not so much in need of the promise and potential, or so attached to our defenses or denial schemes, our senses would have easily picked up the lack of conviction in our partner.

So the difficult-to-accept truth in letting go of resentment about lying is that we first inspect our part in helping to create the conditions for lying to take place. Ask yourself where you feel incomplete and needy. Look at how you have participated in the lies before in your willingness to accept something that was not true. Notice that lies only hurt us in those areas. And notice also that in the areas of completeness in your life, a lie stands out as totally empty and ineffective experience—you don't buy it and it never even lands on you. That should be the clue that you have participated in those other lies that have hurt you in the past. The same could be said about most of our resentments: Where were we participating in what happened?

If you are to stand as source, you are committed to uncover and uproot all of your resentments. This is no easy task, but it is most necessary. Any resentment that has not been removed will easily and quite quickly erode your power and sabotage your effectiveness in life and relationships.

Eliminating Your Resentments: An Exercise

STEP 1: Get a notebook and make a list—an extensive and as exhaustive a list as possible—of all of your resentments against people, principles/rules, and institutions. Take your time and notice that as you start the list, writing some of them will trigger remembrances of other resentments. Go all the way back to your childhood. Try to remember as many of them as possible in the knowledge that resentments most likely (and we might say, all) were never resolved. If you have trouble getting started, think of the small things that happened in the last twenty-four hours and then work backward. And even if you think you have resolved a past resentment, write it down anyway. Leave a space after each name for what you will write in the next two steps.

STEP 2: Next to each person, rule, and institution, write what you resented. What pissed you off or threatened you about it and when was the first time you ever felt that pissed off? Write what comes to mind—cursing is okay and normal. Just go for the gusto.

Step 3: Identify your part. This is a tricky one because to our minds and our memories, it may appear as though the other person was the perpetrator and we had no part in it. But think back to our friend who had been raped: She had no part in causing the event—she was just a young woman. But her part was the story she made up about who she was— and that part of the resentment was hers. She resented her body—herself—for being just what she was. She resented being powerless in the situation.

STEP 4: Now, the big part is to **write down a positive result** that could have been the outcome had you been your best self, your skills of today, your senses, and your power. Again, give yourself permission to think fully. Don't fall victim to the historicity of it all. We are not rewriting history—that cannot happen. We are rewriting your response to it without any resentment.

STEP 5: Last, **make a firm resolve to let go of each resentment.** In some cases, it may be simple to resolve. You can start by drawing a line between your name and theirs—make it as thick as you feel the resentment is for you and then cut the "cord" and burn the paper. In other instances, you may actually want to meet with that person to release them, especially if you have found in your writing that you were way off base in resenting him or her. Give them a call or go meet with them (where it makes sense) and have a beautiful clearing conversation, expecting nothing from them in return. Tell them you made up a story about them and have been holding on to it all these years. No need to say "I'm sorry" as that may sound trite or empty. But let them know that you have moved on to grow up and that is not who you are or how you are now. This is not an opportunity to vent your resentment. You need to be clear that it is all your own crap. This is a beautiful opportunity to start anew with yourself, free from your resentments.

Bobby was a high school egghead and Max was the class bully. Max had size thirteen knuckles and was quick to take anyone out back behind the school and beat them silly. Bobby was afraid of Max but couldn't avoid crossing paths since they rode the same bus. Of course, the inevitable happened one day when Max said in no uncertain terms that Bobby needed to meet him out back. Dutifully Bobby showed up, but to his credit, he used his power tools of verbal ability to convince Max that it would actually damage his reputation to beat up a scrawny nerd like himself. Max saw the wisdom in this line of argument and let him off the hook. But the incident lodged in Bob's unconscious for years to come.

Fast forward in years to the high school class's thirty-fifth reunion. Bob arrived early in the day and decided to stop into the old bar that still was on the corner near the meeting place of the class reunion. While eating his lunch, Bob saw a man at the bar who looked somewhat familiar but couldn't place his face. Figuring him to be about the same age he went over to him and said, "You look familiar, but I can't place your face. I'm here for my thirty-fifth high school class reunion—I used to be Bobby G." The man just grinned and shook his hand. "I used to be Max K. Good to see you Bobby. I hear you're a big deal these days. Well done!" As the two men got to talking,

Bob told Max how much he had feared that meeting and that he had made up a story that he could never be strong and that his intellect was his only skill. Max laughed, "Are you kidding, you are the only kid who had balls enough to stand up to me. I thought you were great!"

Releasing Negative Beliefs

Like releasing our resentments, releasing our negative self-beliefs can be extremely freeing, and doing so is essential for becoming source. Self-concepts (the more popular and acceptable name for our self-beliefs) are totally the invention of our mind. Some are quite serving and helpful while others are impediments to decision-making, risking, and stretching. When you release self-beliefs, focus on the ones that stand in your way. What do you believe to be true about yourself and how did you get those beliefs?

If we asked you to repeat the exercise where you listed them all on a piece of paper and subsequently burned them, you may feel a temporary sense of relief, but before long the old beliefs will be back. That's because you never pulled out the root. What is required in rooting out your negative beliefs is an understanding of how they got there in the first place. In many of the stories we have been telling you, notice that most often an event happened that was interpreted in a certain way. Dan Tocchini is a good friend and a great consultant who is highly effective because of his strongly held self-concepts. But it wasn't always that way for Dan. He had a really rough start as a young adult. He had run-ins with the authorities and was mixed up with the wrong people.

When Dan got clear that living the thug life was not who he was, he had to change a lot of beliefs about himself. He replaced each of his negative thoughts with something positive he believed about his true self. The net result is the strong consultant we see today. Dan does a lot of work with young men in prisons. He recently was describing an incident where he had been challenged by some tough young inmates saying "you don't understand us—you're a rich white dude." Dan never got defensive but rather said thanks for the honesty. "You're right, I don't have the experience you have, and I am a white man, though I might not be as wealthy as you assume. But let me ask you, is it possible that if you told me about your life and I listened well, that I might have a better chance of understanding?" What followed was a deep and honest exchange. The key distinction here is that because Dan had no limiting negative self-concepts, he was able to listen to the inmate's concern without getting defensive or feeling threatened. They were just being straight and honest with him and he met that honesty with his own.

In order to get to the level of effectiveness that Dan shows, we need an actual practice of how to release negative and limiting beliefs. Letting go is clearing the past so you can move forward. Learn to let go by clearing negative energy and forgiving yourself and others. Simply put, when we hang on to the past, it's blocking us from moving forward.

Stuck = Limiting Beliefs + Refusing to Let Go

Do you ever feel stuck like you just can't go forward? Our limiting beliefs hold us back, and we can't go forward if we get stuck on a limiting belief. So how do we stop doing this so we can move forward?

The answer is letting go. *Clearing is getting rid of things that don't serve you and letting go of your attachment to them.* Think about Marie Kondo (the organizing consultant)—tons of people are benefitting from literally clearing out the things that hold them back. You could have a need to clear with another person, with material items, or with yourself. Ask yourself the following questions:

- What have you held on to that held you back? How about this week?

- How does it feel when you hold on?

- What limiting beliefs do you have as a result?

- How would it feel if that thing no longer held you back?

That is the power of clearing and letting go. Clearing is an action you can take to let go of either a thought, a relationship, or a limiting belief that is holding you back. When you clear with another person, you forgive them. No one has to be right. And you propose a solution for going forward. Forgiving is a powerful process of **giving** back the status a person once had **before** they did whatever it was that caused your resentment. While the event is never forgotten or erased, you make a conscious choice to release it and let it go.

It no longer has any power over you and no longer rents space in your mind. That is what we mean by totally letting go.

You can also clear with yourself. Notice how your limiting beliefs are getting in your way. For example, what if you believe, "I believe that I suck at business and everyone is out to get me. I can't get past that and start a new business. I'll never have a successful business if I don't trust people and think I'm a failure." That would be limiting, right? Can you see in that position that there are several limiting beliefs in play? Your beliefs are your interpretation. Beliefs are not facts—they are just interpretations. And you can make a choice to change them. This is a new way of being—in every moment, we make a choice of how to interpret the facts. What if you were to shift your interpretation and your beliefs about something? Instead of believing that you are not worthy of abundance, believe that you are!

What stands behind your ability to let go of a limiting belief is your ability to forgive yourself for that "thing" that happened that resulted in your adopting the limiting or negative belief in the first place. We are often our own harshest critics and are often unforgiving of ourselves.

The thing that so often stands in our way of true success and happiness is our resistance to letting go. When you let go, you shift your interpretation of the facts, you forgive others or yourself, and you make a choice to move forward. No longer will you allow the past to make you believe that things won't change. "The only way to move forward is to let go and complete the past." – Chris Lee, transformational trainer and coach.

Steven Pressfield's masterful book *The War of Art*[10] is one of the best looks at resistance we can find. He talks about *resistance* as if it were the enemy, some person or thing that is out to get us. Pressfield says, "Most of us have two lives. The life we live and the unlived life within us. Between the two stands Resistance." *Resistance* shows up as procrastination, self-doubt, and fear. Later he continues, "Resistance is directly proportional to love [your passion for your calling or higher purpose]. If you are feeling massive *resistance*, the good news is, it means there's tremendous love there too. If you didn't love the project that is terrifying you, you wouldn't feel anything. The more *resistance* you experience, the more important your unmanifested

---

10 Steven Pressfield, *The War of Art: Break Through the Blocks and Win Your Inner Creative Battles.* (New York: Black Irish Entertainment, 2002).

art/project/enterprise [life] is to you—and the more gratification you will feel when you finally do it."

Pain and Suffering Are Transformative

As we are writing this book, our entire world has been thrown into a crisis precipitated by the COVID-19 virus. It is a real and present danger that has had serious and even fatal consequences, and one that has engulfed the world faster than any government, agency, or force could contain. As of this writing, it has caused immense hardship and deep economic disruption. Many friends and, we admit, even we, are feeling a form of pain and suffering as a result.

Nothing we knew has fully prepared us for dealing with this. Oh, certainly there have been a dozen apocalyptic movies about viruses where the hero/heroine had too little time to find the remedy before the human race was eliminated. And there is that 2015 TED Talk[11] by Bill Gates that seems so prophetic now. But the bottom line is that we (our countries, the World Health Organization, and each of us personally) were not prepared for this pandemic, nor have we even begun to recognize the full ramifications of it.

What the fields of psychology and theology have taught us about dealing with feelings of being totally trapped inside our own experience of crisis is that crisis actually produces a state of pain —various forms of pain like mental anguish, fear, frustration, anger, disillusionment, and despair—but pain in every sense of the word. We often feel these emotions physically in our bodies and minds. And over the centuries of studying and working with similar painful crises, the sages have come to a few conclusions about how to "deal" with what has been named impasse, soul suffering, and the dark night of the soul (I have written three books on the last of those topics[12]).

The first and foremost of these suggestions for "dealing" is that we need to be able to sit with the pain and discomfort. If we are unable to be present

---

11 Bill Gates, "The next outbreak? We're not ready," TED Talks, 2015, https://www.ted.com/talks/bill_gates_the_next_outbreak_we_re_not_ready?language=en.

12 Kris Girrell, *Wrestling the Angel: The Role of the Dark Night of the Soul in Spiritual Transformation* (Andover, MA: Kindle Direct Publishing, 2015). Other books on the topic are *Leadership Gold* (2018) and *Stations in the Night* (2019).

to the pain and the physical reality of our impasse, we will try to deny what is really happening and become unable to do a thing about it. In other words, ducking and covering in an attempt to wait it out, or numbing and drugging it away not only creates further pain, but renders us helpless and clueless about what to do. When, however, we recognize our pain as a reality, we are able to begin to heal it. We need compassion and forgiveness, largely from ourselves.

Granted, you have felt pain before. That is not the question. Did you allow yourself to experience the pain, the hopelessness inside that pain, and did you find a way to comfort yourself in that darkness? This is what we see as practicing self-compassion. So how will you deal with this learning moment in world history? Will you let in the fear, despair, and pain enough to learn how to self soothe? Or will you try to be the hero and provide comfort to others without knowing what it really means to feel it yourself? During this pandemic, in fact just as we were about to go into publishing, both of us experienced deeply painful events, something that neither of us likes, given that we are both controlling personality types. One was chronic and on-going in nature—the diagnosis of a recurrence of cancer—and the other was an acute one-time event—the premature birth and death of a child. These painful realities, and the necessary grieving process that currently accompanies them, beckon us to follow our own advice.

When my doctor said the word cancer while reading the results of my most recent biopsy, I literally didn't hear the end of the sentence. My mind started spinning with thousands of thoughts and questions: "I thought we beat this. This is how my friend Richard started and he didn't survive. What are the options?" and so many more. I wanted to immediately dive into research on radiation, hormonal treatments, radical surgery, and naturopathic/metabolic options. But right behind those thoughts came a feeling of sadness bordering on depression. I thought I had won. I still somehow thought I was immortal or invincible. Hadn't the best doctors in the world just used the most advanced treatment available? And then the ego-driven questions hit: Why me? I don't have time for this. My diet is clean; what could have triggered a cancerous reaction? Doing the work of transformation doesn't exempt me from having an ego or from having normal human emotional reactions, but it does allow me to separate the suffering from the pain. My new job has become choosing to experience my emotions, allowing them to do the work on my ego-imposed suffering, and stepping forward anyway.

August was only twenty-two weeks into his developmental journey when he was born. Many of his most vital organs had not matured enough for him to be "viable" on his own. But we are so fortunate to have one of the best NICU (Neonatal Intensive Care Unit) centers in the world and the care of the medical staff was, indeed, world class. Because of COVID, I had made all of the trips to the emergency room (I had been bleeding a lot), prior to his arrival, on my own. And I spent quite a bit of time alone with August as he struggled and fought for his life. My heart grew ten times as I looked down at this little miracle—all 1.23 pounds of him fighting to live. After just four highly emotional days, he chose not to fight anymore, and transitioned on. The grief that hit me, having loved so deeply, so intensely for those four days, was hard to describe. I was not prepared for the power of those feelings that kept washing over me, wave after wave. I cannot deny my emotions even if I wanted to, so my choice has been to adopt August as my teacher. His short-lived struggle and the spirit he imparted with me are teaching me that I am not always in control, that I cannot simply will things away, and that wishing it were different only makes it harder. His spirit calls me to follow my gut instinct and to live in the moment— and the learning is slow.

Before we go any further, let us first say that these two events are not in the least similar. But there is no comparing pain and grief. Nor are our situations comparable (greater or less) than anything you feel or have felt. Pain is pain and grief is individually experienced. It seems like the worst part of that grieving process is that it comes and goes, seemingly at random times and of its own accord. Somewhere in our subconscious, our minds are working on processing it all. Neither of us has control over the onset of grief, only our interpretation of that feeling and our ability to embrace it. This book will be published before either of us knows the final outcome of our stories. But the coincidence of these events, just as we are writing a book subtitled "the only way out is through" is not lost on us! This is life imitating writing. Most importantly, our current experiences and our journeys through the suffering and associated lessons are teaching us deeper compassion for ourselves and others' journeys as well.

Throughout the COVID-19 pandemic, leaders, and entertainers alike were saying "We'll get through this" to which they hastily add, "and get back to normal." That kind of thinking steps over this first element of dealing with the pain. It allows or encourages us to ignore the pain or compartmentalize it and focus our attention on "a better day." That form of escapism serves no one and only delays the growth and development we most need.

But we want to differentiate the suffering from the pain and grief. What if the source of our suffering is not the economic downturn or the fear of the disease or even the potential or real loss of loved ones? What if the suffering is really what we experience as a threat to our ego's presumption that it had everything under control, or that it had counted on a predictable future for which it had such grand plans? These events: cancer, death, loss, physical injury, pandemics and so on are real—they actually happen/happened—and adding more suffering on those painful events, by wishing them to go away, only prevents us from dealing with the transformative power of our pain. The Buddha taught Four Noble Truths. The First was that life consists of pain and suffering. But the Second Noble Truth is that the source of suffering is our personal desires, especially wishing that our current reality were not the case.[13] Stay with the pain and allow it to teach you.

The ugly truth about the transformational journey is that most of us would like the new world of breakthrough without the pain and suffering of breakdown. Pain and suffering demand that we do the hard work. Sitting on the couch or trying to take the easy way demands nothing of us. Taking pills or self-medicating demands nothing of us. Pain and suffering demand that we do the deep inner work—to separate the suffering imposed by our self-will and to let the pain enter us as a pure experience. In truth, this type of pain or grief is the result of our loving deeply. When someone you intensely love dies, the grief you experience is not knowing what to do with that love that no longer has an object. This is the pain that has the power to radically transform us.

---

13 The Four Noble truths are the following: (1) Life consists of pain and suffering; (2) the source of suffering is our selfish desires including material desires; (3) that there is an ending to suffering; and (4) the way to end suffering is the Eightfold Path: Right view, Right thinking, Right speech, Right Action, Right livelihood, Right diligence, Right mindfulness, and Right concentration. Adapted from Thich Nhat Hanh, *The Heart of the Buddha's Teaching: Transforming Suffering into Peace, Joy and Liberation.* (New York: Broadway Books, 1998).

However, if we bypass the pain and the suffering that results from threats to our core beliefs, we will not get to the business of removing the limiting or negative self-thoughts nor break down the irrational belief that the ego holds, that it is superior to everything. Likewise, thoughts of a bright future of "making it big" (or whatever) may well be based on feelings and beliefs of not being enough, of not being successful right now. When a crisis threatens our hopes of something better, we are faced with that ugly underlying negativity. We are forced to admit that we are not in control of the universe. That is what hurts!

Underpinning all of our work in transformation is letting go of the past and, in particular, forgiving and/or having compassion for ourselves and others for the hurts we have experienced. It may be challenging for you to do this, and it may be helpful to do this work with a buddy or partner (or coauthor, in our case), because it requires a high degree of objectivity. This is very pragmatic work and we suggest taking on the following exercises before moving on with the book.

Who Are You Angry With?

Human forgiveness is not doing something but discovering something— that I am more like those who have hurt me than different from them. I am able to forgive when I discover that I am in no position to forgive! The timing will never be right, so decide to do it now.

- Where are you harboring anger?

- Who are you angry with?

Make a list of those you are most affected by in this moment. People in your immediate world – your family, relationships, and coworkers. And people in your life.

What Forgiveness Is NOT

Forgiveness is a very spiritual experience and in and of itself will transform you. In their book *Experiencing Spirituality: Finding Meaning through Storytelling*,[14] Ernest Kurtz & Katherine Ketcham address what forgiveness is and is not. While we highly recommend reading their book, there are several key distinctions about forgiveness that we use that come from the descriptions Kurtz and Ketcham laid out:

- Forgiveness is not **amnesia** – forgiving and forgetting may be akin, but they are two different acts. Forgiveness does not require forgetting, nor can one forgive that which has been forgotten. Forgiveness is a gift given with full memory of what has happened. When have you confused these two? When have you forgiven AND remembered?

- Forgiveness is not **acquittal** –finding a person to be guiltless, blameless, without responsibility for what happened. How often have you refused to forgive a person because you feared they would see it as acquittal?

- Forgiveness is not **achievement** – an award given to the most deserving. It is not earned, nor can it be. Forgiveness is an unearned gift, freely given, without regard to merit. Do you force others to earn your forgiveness? What does this do to your relationships?

- Forgiveness is not **approval** – To forgive another's action is not to condone the act. Can you divorce the two concepts? Or does self-righteousness drive your decisions?

- Forgiveness is not **understanding.** There is a saying that to understand is to forgive, but that is an error. You must forgive *in order to* understand. *Until you forgive, you defend yourself against the possibility of understanding.* If you forgive, you may indeed still not understand, but you will be ready to understand, and that is the definition of grace. What is one thing today that you don't understand, but are ready to forgive?

---

14 Ernest Kurtz and Katherine Ketcham, *Experiencing Spirituality: Finding Meaning through Storytelling* (New York: Tarcher/Penguin, 2014).

- Forgiveness is not **acquiescence**. It is not a license that reads: "Do whatever you like in the future, and it will be okay." Does this speak to you? When have you acquiesced, thinking that you were forgiving? You are not a doormat!

What Forgiveness Is

Forgiveness is knowing acceptance of the person, an acceptance that inspires change rather than waiting for it to happen. Forgiveness is something that is **"given,"** not only in English, but also in French ("Par-donner"), Spanish ("Per-donar"). Forgiveness **must start with self.**

The term self-forgiveness implies that this is a solitary act completed in isolation from others. On the contrary, according to University of Seattle research, the process is a long one, not entirely of one's own doing, which involves *a radical shift in one's way of moving in the world.* The initial experience is an emerging awareness that something is fundamentally wrong about one's life and a feeling of estrangement from self and others. As forgiveness is gradually embodied, one moves toward feeling at home in the world.

Self-forgiveness always takes place in the context of some variation of loving relationships with others. Forgiveness is not an act nor attitude, but *discovery.* That discovery can take place only in a forgiving environment. Think of being in a loving relationship. Would you give your lover a present of a pile of manure? Of course not. But that is precisely what you are doing as long as you have not forgiven yourself. You are giving an unforgivable being as your gift to this relationship, and who would want that? Self-forgiveness involves a shift from self-estrangement to a feeling of being at home with the self, a shift that can take place and indeed be facilitated only in such an environment. *To attain self-forgiveness requires seeking out settings where forgiveness flourishes, situations in which participants are honestly open about their faults and failings.*

"We forgive when we give up attachment to our wounds".– Lewis Hyde

"Forgiveness is giving up hope of having had a better past". – Anne Lamott

Such "letting go" is not intellectual. People think that they've forgiven themselves or somebody else when they've just figured out why they did what they did. But that is not forgiveness. *Understanding is in the head; forgiveness is a surrender of the heart.*

Many urge us to forgive, some claim forgiveness, and a few actually forgive. Lip service, however, is not action. Perhaps all of the talk, rather than action, is based on a lack of understanding but it still amounts to no actual action.

When I decided to let go of my resentment of my father for the abuse of my childhood, I called him to make it real. But after I told him, "I forgive you, dad," his response was "I forgive you too." I hung up the phone just seething with anger at his response. But when I told Andrew about the conversation, he asked, "Did you call to forgive him or did you call because you wanted to hear him say that he was sorry?" In that moment I released the pain, and actually forgave my father—the abuse no longer owned me and was finally let go.

Forgiveness Exercise

Identify three people that you get to forgive. It may be for something small (i.e., missing a call, something that triggered you) or something big (i.e., being purposely hurtful). Rather than sell out on this person, hold them high. This is not easy to do if you have not done the work of transformation. And if you cannot find an instance that triggered you, identify three people who you have failed or triggered in some way. Create an opportunity for forgiveness.

1. Identify the three people.

2. Have an "energetic" conversation about what you want to say to practice.

3. Prepare yourself to be in a conversation of forgiveness without any attention to how they react.

4. Have an actual conversation with them, knowing that you are completely independent of their response. Have an honest conversation with them. Identify what you need to forgive *them* for and what you need to forgive *yourself* for in that situation.

5. Take notes and reflect on the feelings inside during and after the forgiveness exercise.

An actual conversion, while supportive to this process, is not necessary. The act of forgiveness is letting go in your own heart. Our friend Bruce was estranged from his father and decided that it would be a huge growth point to seek him out and forgive him. He prepared the flow of the conversation and was totally prepared for whatever his father would throw at him and was entirely ready to let go. He went to a place where he knew he could find his father, but when his dad got there, he refused to talk with Bruce. Bruce felt that he had failed in his effort, yet found, on reflection and some coaching, that the forgiveness had happened when he prepared to meet his dad. Forgiveness has nothing to do with the other person—it is a gift that is given free of attachments and expectations.

Forgiving and letting go are the essential characteristics of having compassion. But compassion has to start with ourselves as well. Each time we let in the pain and heal it, we are able to be more real in experiencing the next level of suffering underneath that one. We get to a level of self-worth and self-acceptance where we can embrace the pain and despair fully—without denying it. This is not a matter of "cowboying up" and toughing it out. It is, instead, a time to be gentle with yourself, to allow yourself to feel the pain and meet it at its source. Forgive the past and begin to accept who you are as a human. Self-love and self-care are to be administered with the same tenderness that you would give your ill child. You would hold that child tightly on your lap, rocking her gently, telling her how much you loved her, and staying there just as long as is needed. We will come back to forgiveness when we get to the final section of the book.

The amazing thing about suffering with and through pain is that it gives us access and understanding to that reality. By sitting with our pain, we are able to transform it and transform our most inner beliefs. It moves us to an entirely new and more whole "come from" for ourselves and others. Perhaps the most important lesson of suffering is that you cannot give compassion to others if you do not know suffering on your own part or have not practiced acceptance and compassion for yourself first. Anything you try to do as compassionate without your own self-compassion will be patronizing and coming from a position of privilege. No one wants to be patted on the head and told "Oh, poor thing, this will pass, better days are coming," by someone who has no clue of what pain and suffering actually feels like.

Certainly, we are not contending that the current global crisis is a good thing in its ability to drive transformation. But neither are we saying that it is inherently bad. Remember, our interpretations make things good and bad; situations and events are neutral. The power lies in our ability to discover what is at source for our interpretations and to choose another interpretation based on our having let go of the old limiting beliefs.

One last word on the COVID-19 crisis. We are excited by the possibility this pandemic raises. It has the power to transform our society, our governments, and our way of being with the planet —if we embrace it. But that is the key: We as a people must do everything we can to ensure that the lessons this pandemic crisis presents are learned, taken to heart, and implemented in a way that moves humankind forward. We have the power to create the "new normal." As leaders, each in our own sphere, our mandate is to move our collective forward toward healing, lest we retreat to our ways of being that existed before the pandemic. But saying we are excited by those possibilities in no way means that we step over the personal loss of loved ones —even family members—who died because of this disease. Pain and suffering are transformative, but only if and when we let the pain in and allow it to do its transformative work of dashing our egoist beliefs. When we put the thought that we are separate and distinct from each other aside, we are able to focus our awareness on the plight of our most vulnerable siblings as people of this earth.

Masks and Shadows

How open and vulnerable you are will be reflected in how open and vulnerable others will be. Breakthrough demands vulnerability. As long as you or your friend has a deflector shield up and armed, neither of you will get where you need or want to go. It is like you are wearing a mask and that mask has to come off. Your mask is made up of two sides: an outside (facing the world) and an inside (facing you). This part concerns your mask.

The outward side of our mask is your "resume," your great qualities, and accomplishments that we think are our identity. It is covered with answers to the cocktail party question of "Who are you?" The outside of the mask is dressed up and covered with pretty images, words, and experiences. It is bright and beautiful and a source of pride—certainly all the things we want to tell others about. *AND* it includes a little bit about the fact that you have done this powerful breakthrough work! "Just let me tell you how much I have changed, how much I have gained, and how wonderful my life is since doing the work of transformation!"

The inside of your mask is covered equally as much with images and graffiti. Only these images and thoughts are a bit less desirable. The inside of the mask is like your "bad neighborhood" where you would never invite a friend to come visit. There is graffiti on the walls, fights in the dark alleyways, cars overturned and on fire—you really wouldn't want to go in there alone! They are the parts of us that we would prefer never see the light of day. They are things like guilt and shame about having done something, sadness about being the last kid picked in our younger years, and things like failures and struggles that would never make it to our resume. The inside is just as much a part of our identity as our outside, but we don't want or like that part of us. If we could cut it off, we think, we would be a lot better off. Denying or repressing the inner side of your mask will never get you to and through a breakthrough. Oh, intellectually you will understand the concepts of breakthrough, but you will never get it at the "bone marrow" level.

You may want to work on this: In order for you to really show up to that special person, or be acknowledged for your work in transformation, you need to be actively working on embracing the inside of your mask, because it is only when others feel your openness to you owning your inner "shadow self" that they will be willing to trust that the same is possible for them. It is only when you are vulnerable that you give permission for others to be the same. We all know there is a shadow there, but most of us are afraid of dealing with those demons.

The key here is that you cannot take something from the inside of your mask and put it on the outside (Like: "See how well I am embracing my demons and my shadow!"). The evidence that you are doing that inner work is that your friends will experience that vulnerable energy from you. Others are the litmus paper or the barometer through which you will know that you are doing the work. While this sounds like it is about you doing the inner work, it is all about that other person "getting it" that you are doing the work. You may never really know the truth about yourself (ego wants to believe non-truths as truth) without the feedback from others.

The Pure Power of Love and Vulnerability

It is no accident that all of the great mystics and sages of all times have said the love is the answer—and that love is the source. Yes, of course love is the coming together on a physical plane that creates new life, but that is not what they, the sages, mean. Only love can understand great wisdom. Or, if you prefer the corollary, without great love, wisdom and knowledge will be slaughtered, misinterpreted, and used for its own gain.

To quote a famous passage (that may be quite overused and mostly misunderstood), "Love is patient and kind; love does not envy or boast; it is not arrogant or rude. It does not insist on its own way; it is not irritable or resentful;it does not rejoice at wrongdoing, but rejoices with the truth. Love bears all things, believes all things, hopes all things, and endures all things." That is quite a mouthful! And while the author is describing the subject love as if it were a person, it is a great description of what love as source results in.

Without love, knowledge becomes a power tool and is used as a force to separate and marginalize others. For eons, only the ruling class had access to knowledge and they kept it that way to keep the masses under their control. Without love as the foundation, our speaking and conversations are just so much noise—all "I this" and "I that." Without love, anything we possess will become ego-stoking narcissism (all about us). And without love as our source anything we do—even the most noble of efforts—will be done for the wrong reasons and result in a relatively small impact or nothing at all.

But love is just the opposite. The great theologian, Paul Tillich, said that love was the "ground of our being." Love is not a thing we do or a place to get. It is the source of all things and it is the force which pulls all things together and unites them. More than anything else, *Typhoon Honey* is a book about how to get to the source of love that unites all things. So we need to take a moment to explore love and its action verb form, loving.

The first characteristic of love is that it has no conditions or boundaries to it. Perhaps we first experience this quality of love when, as an infant, we locked eyes with our mothers for the first time. That one gaze—while being held close to her breast, while our hearts were still circulating her blood—that moment cemented in place an understanding of what unconditional love felt like. So, somewhere, deeply embedded in our psyches, is a memory of the feeling and effect of love. But that only scratches the surface of what love is. Because soon after that magical moment, our brains took over the learning process and overshadowed the magnificent learning power of our hearts. Only now, in the 21st century is research catching on to the fact that our hearts are an integral part of the nervous system and of our ability to learn, receive, and process information. We may be close to the day when the field of psychology understands that our heart—the center for love—is also the center of wisdom.

If love is the ground of our being, then the ground of our being is receiving and compassionate. Love does not judge the other but rather accepts and has compassion for the other. That does not mean that you roll over and play dead to abuse or accept inappropriate behavior on the part of another person. It means that when correcting their behavior, you come from a place of understanding how painful it must be to be lashing out and how painful it must have been to grow up and into a state of hate or abuse as one's only defense. So, being love-grounded, we lovingly correct; we lovingly stand our ground against violence and abuse. It is difficult but it is the way of love.

And love is immensely powerful. I once saw a leader, who was being berated by another person, stand closely in front of his attacker and say, "I can love you harder than you can hate me." It was totally disarming of the other person's rage. In addition, love is hopeful. But not hoping in (something like a savior or a favor) or hoping for (something like a brighter future), love is hopeful—as in full of hope—period. Hope is a state that requires nothing for its existence. When we are filled with and grounded in love, we have hope, just because love is so powerful.

Now here is the twist: Love makes us vulnerable, and vulnerability is an essential leadership skill. The two go hand in hand. But, becoming source, like leadership, requires being vulnerable and taking risks. If your intention is to take on your life as the *source* of your life and your results, then that involves risking and being vulnerable. There is no risk that does not involve being vulnerable to the consequences.

Vulnerability often suffers from a bad reputation. Most people think of vulnerability as being open to attack and capable of being wounded, which of course are the definitions of vulnerability. But the power of vulnerability is that it creates an openness for the other person to come into our space. If we wish to be loving in our approach to the world and to those around us, and if we live with compassion and understanding of others, that cannot come from a place of superiority. We love with our hearts wide open. Being open and vulnerable, we allow the other person the full freedom to be who and what they are. Vulnerability, like love, has no conditions placed on the other. It is not a matter of being vulnerable if the other person is nice or harmless. That is like saying, "I will love you if you are loveable." Both love and vulnerability are conscious choices made irrespective to the conditions and circumstances surrounding us. But just as we said about love, it does not mean we get to be naïve about where and when we are vulnerable.

We are not suggesting that you be totally defenseless in this process. You are powerful beyond your own beliefs and there is a huge difference between someone who is weak and vulnerable because of that weakness and a powerful, confident person who understands she is source for her experience and from source chooses to love unconditionally and be vulnerable enough to create a space wherein others can come into that love. Think of it like this: Have you ever known someone who was so gracious and humble that you had no other choice than to be humble with her and in response to her? Of course. Just as you know someone who is so abrasive or pushy that your first instinct was to be abrasive and pushy in response. Love and vulnerability are the same. It is possible to be loving in such a way that there is no other possible response from others than to be loving. It is possible to be vulnerable in such a way that there is no other possibility for others than to be vulnerable in response. People will naturally mimic that which they see. Psychologists call it the "mimetic response," and we were born with it. If you generate unconditional love, you will get it in return. If you generate unconditional vulnerability, you will get that in return as well.

You will need to continually have your senses alive and be present to what is happening. As a result, you would know not to walk into a hostile situation and simply turn on your love vibes. However, it is possible to disarm a violent situation by being a source of love and compassion. You just need to be aware of what is happening. In no way are we suggesting that you put yourself in danger. You get to employ all of your skills and senses at all times— that is what we mean by being present. By being present, you can assess the situation and know whether this is one in which you defend your safety or one in which your love and vulnerability will diffuse the volatility. Be safe! However, what we are suggesting is that our default mode should be love and vulnerability, as those two are the most powerful forces known to humankind.

I once worked for a very insightful CEO who brought the team together at the beginning of the sales cycle for the annual pep talk. Before speaking he wrote five words on the board: Money, Customers, Knowledge, Wisdom, Love. He then asked, "How will we know we are successful?" It wasn't just making money because money comes and goes, and it wasn't because they had captured customers either. He said perhaps, then it is the knowledge gained from their customers, but that too is fleeting. And while wisdom—the application of knowledge—is perhaps the best, ultimately, we will know we are successful "if we can walk away from this experiment called life having loved each other and everyone we have come in contact with." And this was a financial firm where we don't normally find the word love discussed as the prime operator!

One last safety valve we will add here is that since life is a relationship game, our suggestion is that you not play the game of life alone. Do everything in relationship. Build relationships with those around you. Go into the world in partnership. Deal with adversity and hostility by having your team around you. If you think that love and vulnerability are powerful, you should see it done with a team or group—the force is exponential.

Not Doing It Alone

It is a curious phenomenon to notice that we often attempt to do things alone. Why is it that when we are faced with our most pressing issues, we tend to retreat inside and go solo when our nature is to be in relationship. Early in our evolution—several hundreds of thousands of years ago—humans found both safety and strength in community. We are not evolutionarily strong enough to have survived as solo individuals. In fact it is only in recent history, literally in the last century, where we began to prize being an individual.

We often can see in others that which we fail to see in ourselves. In studying our two closest evolutionary relatives—the chimpanzees and the bonobo monkeys—we see a stark example of love and the importance of not doing life alone. The chimps, it seems, are much more like loners in that once the young chimpanzees reach adolescence, they start becoming more independent and venturing out alone to explore. By contrast, the bonobo are extremely social, continuing to live in communities, and appear to be far more caring about each other—even in their sexuality, where the bonobo face each other and often stroke their partner's face. But when we look at their overall social patterns the more social bonobos do not fight and appear to be thriving while their cousins, the chimpanzees, who are more individualistic, territorial, and aggressive, are dying off at a much higher rate. It seems that when we join together and work in groups, the competition increases our survival.

When you decide to stand as source you cannot stand alone by yourself. You cannot nor should not do any of this on your own. It would be a violation of your nature as a human. As we have discussed that in the physical world "everything is connected," the same is true in the psychological world.

We only learn how to be vulnerable, take risks, be committed, and forgive inside the container of a relationship. Think of the last time you learned one of those lessons—vulnerability, risking, making commitments, and so on, and write them down. As you look at your list, how many of those were done in relationships and how many of those were done alone? Taking that a step further, of the ones that were done alone, how many of those were profound for you versus the ones that were done in relationships? The lessons that teach us the most and allow us to take the deepest cuts on our understanding of ourselves most often are those that have been learned in the context of a relationship. Certainly, you can make a commitment to yourself or take personal risks with regard to the physical environment, but those have relatively little power to alter your world or the results you can produce. You live in a world populated by over seven billion other humans. And within those billions of people, you have relationships with multiple circles: your family of origin, your local community or neighborhood, your work team and company, and your church, synagogue, ashram, or spiritual group. And you have what we might call relatedness with thousands of others through circles of interest, online communities and social networks and so on. To think that you function in a vacuum would be ludicrous.

If you want to know what you are sourcing, take a look at your circle of closest friends.

Write them down and take a close look. Who are they for you? Are they inspiring you or cheering you on? Are they dragging down or holding you back? Are they happy or unhappy with their current lot in life? These will be the first indications of what you are sourcing for your life.

Then take a look at how you interact with them. Are you afraid to tell them how you feel, or who you really are? Are you able to let down your guard with them or to have those really hard conversations? Are you able to cry with them? How often do you talk with them? Are you being your word with them and are they being their word with you? Do you take time to tell them that you love them (not how much because love isn't something that is measurable), but just that you love and value them?

Do you really know their love language? As Gary Chapman points out in his book *The 5 Love Languages*,[15] each of us has a different "language" for expressing and giving love. Show them your love by acts of service for them or spending time with them, touch, or whatever their language is.

Once you uncovered how to share yourself and learn from those people you love the most, step two is to take this out one layer, then two and three levels out until you get to the random person you interact with at the grocery store. What is it that you want to leave that person feeling about themselves and about the world? How are you going to communicate with them so that they see the world in that way?

It takes perhaps a bit of vulnerability to fully express your love to your family and friends. But why stop there? Take a risk with your friends, associates, and coworkers to tell them that you love them as well. Love in its purest sense has no demands on the other person. It is simply what we are designed to do and how we are meant to be. Thank people for being who they are —not for what they did. Love is the first step in widening your family, your tribe, and your belongingness.

---

15 Gary Chapman, *The 5 Love Languages: The Secret to Love That Lasts.* (Chicago, IL: Northfield Publishing, 1992-2015).

With a solid network of close friends and cohorts, you begin to tap into the energy of the universe. Since the universe—the source of abundance and power—is composed of all living things, your ever-widening circle or tribe is a localized version of the larger universe. If the energy of one person (you) is powerful, then the combined energy and intentions of twenty, forty, or a hundred people is exponentially greater. Think of a time when you were dancing by yourself in the bathroom in front of a mirror. Then think of a time when you were dancing with a group of fifty or one hundred others. What was the difference between those two experiences? By yourself, you may just be in your little groove having some fun, but in a big crowd of dancing, partying people, letting loose all of their joy and energy, the feeling is closer to ecstatic.

Everything is connected— both in the physical world and in the psychological world. You are as much a part of me as I am a part of you. "We" becomes more powerful each time it is spoken or experienced, because each time we act or speak as "we," we create an ever-expanding circle of interdependence. In being or becoming source, we get to understand our place in the circle of humankind. We understand that our intention is shared by hundreds or thousands of others seeking the same thing. And we feel their energy just as we would feel the energy in a room full of others dancing together with us. Life is not meant to be lived in solitude and standing as source cannot be done in isolation. We all are in this lifeboat together.

As humans, we start out on this life journey as infants where we are highly dependent on others for our food, safety, and belonging. Then as we mentioned, we move into a time where we become independent, where we learn to identify ourselves as separate and unique. We often refer to this as our self-concept, and that often contains many beliefs carried over from our childhood when we were just small and not terribly powerful. But by gaining skills and amassing accomplishments, we eventually see ourselves as self-sufficient.

Unfortunately, many people stop there. Popular psychology teaches us that we have arrived when we become fully independent. We have a sense of "can do" and take pride in all that we can accomplish on our own. *This is the grand illusion of life!* We begin to understand that the goal is in sharing our gifts, talents, and strengths with others. As adults we understand that our survival is in the combined talents and energies of all of us together. Fully mature adults accept that we were designed to be in service and in relationship with others of our kind. And in fact, fully mature adults recognize that our true nature is to live in relationship with the entire world —the physical world, the planet, and nature, as well as other humans—as an integral part of that world. Our sustenance comes from the planet and its natural resources. Our emotional well-being comes from being in relationship with others. We are interdependent.

Interdependence and Codependence

Interdependency does not mean that we only have self-worth if someone else says so. We do not wrap our self-worth up in others' opinions. It means that we have self-worth when we are able to give our full, our complete, and mature selves, to others. It is often said that marriage, or a committed relationship, is a 50/50 deal—that we "complete" each other. But mature interdependence is really a 100/100 relationship. We bring a complete and fully developed independent self to the other, and they bring their full self to us. Anything less would be what psychologists call "codependent." Codependency (a complex issue that is beyond the scope of this book) simply means that, however functional or dysfunctional our family of origin was, it was where we formed the bulk of our self-concepts about relationships. We learn that we are a piece of that system—like a piece of a pie. Then, when we leave that family, we first attempt to find another system or relationship where we can find completion—the rest of the pie! Codependency is living life from the perspective of needing others (or the world) to fulfill your empty places, your unformed parts, and your incompletions. In short, you need others' approval to feel okay.

Interdependence, the 100/100 form of relationship, means that we have completed the pie on our own. We have resolved our issues and sense of incompletion we first learned in our family of origin. We no longer need someone else to "complete" us. Rather we find the complementary aspects and acknowledge the other for the complete being that they are.

So, the work behind our ability to stand as a source in life is that of becoming complete and whole as a person, then learning our role as an integral element of our universe. We simply cannot partner with the abundance in the universe if we think that it is the universe's job to complete us and fill us up. Becoming and being the source of our lives requires a symbiotic relationship between us and the universe around us. The more complete you are, the stronger that relationship is. The more interdependent we learn to be, the stronger and more powerful that partnership becomes.

Here is an assignment:

Create a list of every aspect of your life that you are living at 100 percent. Then create a list of anything where you are looking for outside validation or "completion." List three people you see as living their life at 100 percent across the board or at least in the areas where you want to be 100 percent. Contact each of those people and build a mentoring relationship with them —not a codependence—but rather a way in which you can learn from them how to take your life to one hundred in that area.

Section Three

The Tools of Becoming Source

Kris Girrell & Candace Sjogren

–5–

Accountable, Responsible, and Source

The Difference between Accountable and Responsible

Accountability and responsibility are two sides of the same coin. They both deal with the same way of being and are the foundations of becoming source. Accountability could be thought of as "count-on-ability." Accountable people own their actions and results. When they make a commitment, others know that they can count on it happening. Responsibility is the ability to respond (not react) to any given situation from one's own values and commitments. People who react are controlled by their environment. But responsible people evaluate the situation and respond to it in terms of their intentions. Our friend Michael Strasner says, "To be responsible is to be the sole, uncontested author of one's life."

Accountability and responsibility have nothing to do with blame and fault and everything to do with success. Accountable people measure their effectiveness in terms of their results. And accountable leaders measure their effectiveness in terms of their team's results. So when accountable people see that the results are off target from their intended outcome, they take responsibility for the situation, knowing that they are the ones who must alter their actions and intentions in order to correct it.

The foundation of accountability and responsibility is having a clear intention. Everything else flows from that. Once you have become clear about your goal and intention, you will begin to take responsibility for that outcome. In fact, you will feel as if you have no choice other than to do what is needed as the next right step. You have no choice because your vision and intention demand it of you. After all, you said this was what you wanted and intended for your life. Now you get to own it fully.

Accountability Starts with Forgiveness

Once you have begun owning your world, your results and your role as the source of your life, you recognize that there are parts and pieces that are not aligned with how you intend your life to be. Most of that comes from the residual effects of past experiences that you have not yet resolved. And resolving past issues requires forgiveness. Someone (there is some dispute as to the actual source) wiser than we are once said that forgiveness is giving up all hope of having a different or better past!

Until you forgive your past events you cannot and will not be freed from being the victim of that past event. Earlier, we described a person who had been raped in her past. While she was in actuality a victim in that event, the history and the meaning she took about herself kept her locked in that victim role. Forgiving her rapist was the most difficult thing she ever attempted. But she recognized that as long as she saw him as the rapist, she saw herself as the victim of rape. Letting go of that view of perpetrator and victim was the only way to be freed from her past interpretations.

We know of people who have forgiven the drunk driver who hit and killed their mother or son. We have heard of people who have forgiven former business associates who stole millions from them. The list of unthinkable grievances is as varied as you can imagine, but in each case, the person recognized that the only way to live a free life of source was to forgive the grievance and let it go. Holding on to the victim story kept them trapped in that story and that role of the victim.

Forgiveness is the most powerful tool in your arsenal—with the possible exception of love. But forgiveness is love and compassion applied to another person. Our friend who forgave the woman who killed his mother by driving drunk realized that she was living a life of total pain, knowing that her one night of bad choices, of drinking and driving, had taken a life and had robbed a family of their mother. He imagined the tortured life she was living and found compassion in his heart for her. But he did not contact her to solve her life problem. Rather he knew that until he forgave her and felt some compassion for her life, he could not be free to live his life in full love and abundance—it would always be lessened by holding on to the anger and resentment.

Accepting the Position of Source

Okay, it's time to go to work. Make sure you have your journal nearby because this section is filled with questions for reflection. Take your time with this section and don't rush through. The questions are meant to further your thinking and experience of this material.

In the first chapter of this book, we discussed the importance of understanding the laws of the physical world. The reason was that if you are to stand as source of your life and your future, your way of being is, of necessity, one with that universal source. Essentially the sum of those laws would be what we call the laws of cause and effect. Standing as source means that you are the cause. Everything you see around you and everything that shows up are the effects of your being that cause or the choices you have made. Standing as source means recognizing that you are not only aligned with the source, the universe, but that you are a part of that universal source. You understand that the universe is the infinite source of everything and that, as part of that source, you have infinite capacity to source the outcomes you intend. The universe is non-discriminating and simply produces the effect that you set in motion as the cause by virtue of your choices. The effects are, in simple terms, just feedback. If you don't like the feedback, then you simply observe, shift, and choose again.

Write down ten things that have happened in the last week or so that you didn't like. Notice that your natural tendency is to blame someone or something else for your circumstance. Identify at least one new interpretation of the same event where you are the source of it. Having trouble making this leap? Great! Read on.

Observe

Recognizing that the laws of cause and effect are coming from your way of being and the choices you have been making, step one is to become aware of whatever it is that you are being and doing. Ask yourself what is your way of being? What are the beliefs that you are holding on to? Observe the results—the effects—and you can extrapolate into your way of being. If negativity surrounds you, then your way of being has a negative charge. If your feedback results are showing up as great barriers and obstacles, how might you be resisting your efforts that you have produced those roadblocks? Stopping to observe yourself provides the opportunity to "just notice" what is happening around you as clues to your way of being.

Shift

Shifting means altering your being—where you are coming from—to a more powerful and positive stand. Shifting allows you to alter the source of who you are and how you are behaving, acting, talking, and interacting with the world around you. Shifting allows you to reground yourself in the abundance of the universe, knowing it to be the infinite source of all things. In order to shift, ask yourself what your beliefs are that resulted in the effects that you see? Ask what you believe to be true when you are grounded and one with the universe? When you are completely aligned with and a part of the universe, your state of being is complete abundance. Shift your "come from" and you shift the results. Change your language and you can change the outcomes. In Jotina Buck's book, *Change Your Language, Change Your Life*,[16] she suggests changing the language around the tasks in your life. What would happen if instead of saying "I have to go for groceries," you said "I get to go for groceries," or "I am blessed to go for groceries." Remember, you are the source; you are the source. Everything you do, think or say, is the source of what comes next.

---

16 Jotina L. Buck, *Change Your Language, Change Your Life: 30 Enlightenment's to Unlock Unlimited Possibilities*. (CreateSpace Independent Publishing Platform, 2015).

Choose

From your new perspective of source and from this being-ness that you now stand in, you get to make new choices. Previously your choices were limited to only those that you could see from your then state of being. When you have shifted that being to one aligned with the universe and the universe's abundance, you now will see other choices and options. But know that if you do not see different choices, you have not completely shifted! Keep shifting until what you see are the different options, then choose one and go, knowing that if this choice does not produce the results you wanted, then you can choose again; and again. Each time just observe, shift, and choose. For those times you feel backed into the corner, notice what is happening (observe), shift your "come from" and list at least five new options, then choose!

Feedback Is a Gift

Earlier in this book we stated that nearly all of what you see around you can be thought of as feedback. We are now at a point where we can really dig into that. The long and short of understanding feedback is learning to decipher the consequences of our actions so that we can learn from it and move in the right direction. Feedback is information and all information is good information. But what exactly do we mean by feedback?

The simplest answer is to look around. What do you see? Your home, your career, the relationships you have and don't have, your economic status, all of it could be classified as feedback. Take, for example, your career. Suppose you have a great talent but keep ending up on the short list when it comes time for cutbacks or layoffs. Of course, you could believe that it is a matter of last-in-first-out, or perhaps because of your experience you may command a higher salary and thus become a target for cutbacks as the easiest, largest saving. However, we would encourage you to consider how that history of continually being cut is feedback about the way you are or aren't showing up.

People who take this journey seriously start with the belief that there is always something to learn and that within every event there is some good, informative feedback. Once they see that it is information that is useful in learning how to adjust their effort, their way of being or their communication, they suddenly become hungry for more feedback. It is all good, actionable information.

Did you ever notice that some people have huge parties or a ton of names in their address file? They have the same opportunities to make friends as any other person yet their list is larger by an order of magnitudes. Of course, that could be because that person is an extrovert and you think you are a tad on the introverted side. But looking at it from a perspective of feedback, this evidence also tells you that they are doing something that you may not be doing. Or if you are that person, you can see that what you do to attract people clearly works.

Feedback is a way of monitoring how well something worked or did not work. It is the same if you were setting up your LinkedIn account and started posting articles. One thing you might do is to select different types of cover pictures. You start with some with vibrant colors, then try some with cartoon graphics, or news photos. After posting for several months, you could analyze what works best by the number of views and reposts you had for each article. Certainly, you might think that it was the content, but you intentionally conduct this experiment to determine what attracted people more. Just like manufacturing and technology do with products, you conduct A/B testing; you gather feedback.

If you would like to experiment with yourself a little bit, try the following: Change your way of being for one week and see what kind of feedback you get. For example, if you are typically a serious person, spend a week being light and easygoing. If you are typically the one to jump into leadership, spend a week taking the last place in line to let others be first in leading. Think of it like trying on a new suit or dress. But for this little experiment, don't worry so much about how you feel in that other style, just notice. Instead, just gather feedback on how people react to you and notice the results. There's no commitment needed—you just try it on as an experiment.

The difficult application of the principle of feedback is when we claim that everything is feedback. If you got into an argument with your lover, that is feedback. When you are continually frustrated because things seem not to go "your way," that too is feedback. In truth, you cannot have it both ways—that some feedback results are good and useful while other information is the result of outside factors or interference! Either everything is feedback or nothing is. Standing as source is a place of choosing to view everything as information and feedback.

Taking Inventory – An Exercise in Feedback

Take out your notebook because you will need to take a lot of notes.

- Start by listing as much of your current surroundings and conditions as you can.

- List your car, your bank account, your relationship, your family situation, your contact list, your job, your resume items—everything you can think of that are the net results of how you have been showing up. These are your results and symbols of the feedback you are receiving.

- Beside each item place a plus or a minus to indicate that it is either above the desired line of what you would want or a minus sign for those items below the line.

- On a separate page write several paragraphs describing what you did to source those results that are above the line.

- Then do the same for those results that are below the line. What are you doing and how are you showing up as indicated by the results that are lower than your intention?

Tell yourself the truth and really dig into this exercise. You don't have to finish the exercise in one sitting. Keep out your journal and add to it each time you notice something else to add to the plus or minus list. Be an observer of your life and its feedback.

Fractals – How You Do One Thing Is How You Do Everything

In the first chapter, we discussed some of the physical laws with which we not only need to be familiar but by which we play the game of life. There is another scientific and mathematical principle called fractal theory[17] that contends that the part and the whole are identical, or that most complex systems are comprised of self-repeating patterns that are the same as the entire pattern. An easy example of this is looking at a head of cauliflower or a beautiful Romanesco broccoli. If you look at the basic shape and texture of a whole head it has a certain bumpiness distinct to cauliflowers. But if you break off one of the clusters and look at its surface closely it resembles the same pattern as the entire head. If you were to break off one floweret and look at it under a magnifying glass, the floweret also has the same pattern. Fractals are patterns that are the same form no matter how large or small a sample you take.

The reason that this is important is that behavior is also a fractal in much the same way as snowflakes, cauliflowers, and constellations. We humans are physical beings and obey the same laws of nature and science as the rest of the universe. If you were to look at the whole of your life, you would see a pattern of actions and commitments, of things done and things left undone, of successes and face-plants. Looking at the past year, you would probably notice the same pattern. And the same is true of yesterday and just a moment ago. Just like the cauliflower, you would see eventually that in the smallest action or deed, there is that same self-repeating patterned behavior.

The simple explanation is that everything you think, do, or say comes from the same source—your mind and its pattern of beliefs, values, and constructs. Your mind is essentially a collection of stored patterns accumulated over life. Those collected thoughts and values *inform* every action and every decision you make, so that it is highly likely that you will act in the same patterned way.

Our way of expressing this is "how you do anything is how you do *everything*, and how you do everything is how you will do this one thing." For example, a lifetime habit of panicking when being asked to do some "stretching" type of behavior will be reflected in some form of resistance or outright panic at the next time you are challenged to "step up." How a person is responding in the moment reflects how they normally have been

---

17 Here is a simpler explanation of fractals: Khan Academy, "What is a fractal (and what are they good for)?" https://www.khanacademy.org/partner-content/mit-k12/mit-k12-math-and-engineering/mit-math/v/what-is-a-fractal-and-what-are-they-good-for

"doing" life. You can therefore intuit from how you or others are reacting that the reaction is a whole programmed-in pattern, practiced over life, that sits behind why they or we are doing the things we do.

However, this can be just as positive as it is negative. If we can put our habituated pattern on hold for a moment and start a practice of, let's say, choosing a positive direction, then repeat that as often as possible, that new pattern will generalize to life. The truth about humans is that we cannot be in two different states, systems, emotions, or fractals at the same time. Try being relaxed when you are totally tensed up. Try being sad when you are laughing, or vice versa! You can't do it. In the same way, the process of transforming our lives and living is as simple as creating new fractals that repeat into the whole of our lives.

How many times have you noticed that people are happy on sunny days and more down and lethargic on gloomy, rainy days? But what if we want to practice the state of joy? Joy is not a synonym for happy or happiness. Joy is a state of being wherein you are positive about life because you have life, because life is a privilege every day you wake up. Living from joy and gratitude is just a practiced state of being. Unlike the previous statement above that you can't be happy and sad at the same time, you can live in joy even at the funeral of a close friend. Joy does not mean that you are dancing and laughing. Joy means that you have a deep love of life and embrace every moment for the fullness that it is.

Let's Try an Example of Using the "Reverse" Aspect of Fractal Theory

If how you do one thing is how you do everything, then you may also have the ability to start small and build one element of life into a full-fledged way of life. For example: perhaps your current way of life is scattered. Imagine perhaps being an artist whose art is the ability to put concepts and forms together in unique, "artistic" ways. Perhaps, as this artist, your way of being is to have many, *many* things laying out and about your living and creating space, so as to have more "access" to them. But, in our example, let's imagine then that you have grown weary of the feeling of clutter but you feel overwhelmed and confused as to where you can start. Using the principle of fractals, you can start by noticing how all of your life habits are a fractal of that overall pattern of randomized availability of all things—having them all strewn about. Your bathroom is cluttered, the kitchen has a gazillion things on the counter (for ease in cooking, you say), and your bedroom has a couple of dozen pants and shirts hanging on the corners of doors, on doorknobs, and laying about on any or every flat surface (because you have been telling yourself those are out to help put together favored outfits faster).

So let's start small, with just one area. Pick your favorite (in this case non-art) activity. For purposes of this discussion, let's say you love to cook—so we start with the kitchen. Now we want to engage your strength—that which drives all your patterns—creative thinking. Sit in the middle of the kitchen and notice how the design is laid out. Architects are not often cooks, so they may have laid out things in a way that doesn't suit your preparation and cooking of meals. Notice that your "clutter" pattern has certain tools or ingredients in areas where they are most often used. Maybe the cutting boards need to be closer to the refrigerator. Maybe the measuring tools (cup measures and such) are over where the flour and dry ingredients are. What you can do with that awareness is begin rearranging the cabinets and drawers to match where the clutter points and contents are so that everything has a "place" where it is most used. The point here is to make your rearranging and reordering of the area fit you and your style.

Here's the special sauce of this process: because you have done this reordering on your favorite activity (it need not be the kitchen example), your ability to do the same with other subsections of your life will be driven by the *power* of your favorite activity. *When we pair a low-likelihood event with a high-likelihood event, a strong passion or habit, the less likely behavior takes on the frequency and strength of the higher, more powerful event.* It works. And over time, you can gradually build a new fractal cluster of behaviors that infect all other ways of your being. I love baklava—it is my favorite food. When I was studying for the bar exam, a client had sent me this huge box of baklava—about one hundred pieces. So I paired my studies (a low probability event) with having a piece of baklava (high probability event) and following that with a set of crunches (another low probability event). I not only passed the bar on the first attempt but I didn't gain any weight from eating baklava. But on a side note, every time I have baklava, I now have this desire to immediately drop down and do crunches!

126

Rigor, Discipline, and Urgency

Why would we be writing about rigor—mostly defined as rigidity, inflexibility or immoveable— in a book dedicated to creating possibility? The simple, and yet not so simple, answer is that standing as source is not an arbitrary state. To be source of your world and your experience of it requires not simply responsibility or accountability. This demands far more of you. Your vision is no longer a choice you have to make—it is a mandate. Your personal commitment is not a wish or a statement of possibility. In fact, all of the odds may be against your successfully fulfilling that commitment. The "drift" of the world, of others (including friends and family), and of your work life may all be telling you that you are off your rocker, tilting at windmills or just not seeing what they all call "reality."

But having made that commitment, you now put all of your resources to work in supporting your movement in the chosen direction. Your commitment takes on a single-mindedness and, if done correctly becomes an unstoppable force of nature. You are so convinced of the *authority* of your commitment that you become unmovable. Everything you do takes on shades of that commitment. Everything you think or say becomes couched in terms of that commitment and you are unshakable in that stand. So, the definition of being rigidly immoveable and inflexible may in fact fit our needs here. Though inflexible sounds a bit obstinate and stubborn, your rigor requires that level of resolve.

I mentioned before that I had run a marathon. Allow me to explain how rigor and urgency played into that activity. The day I decided to run the Boston Marathon, I was overweight and out of shape. I am not built like a runner. At six feet three and weighing 250 pounds, I looked more like a defensive tackle than a runner. I had not run in ages and even back then the most I had ever accomplished was perhaps a three- or four-mile jog. But that day I was watching the regular runners as they came into the home stretch, rounding the corner of Hereford onto Boylston Street. It is the first time in their twenty-six–mile ordeal that they will see the finish line, some 460 yards away. As I watched, I saw one man come around the corner and, shouting for joy, he did a cartwheel! Imagine: he had just run twenty-six miles and he had the energy and excitement to pull off a cartwheel. My only thought at seeing that was, "I want to know what that feels like." That thought was immediately followed by the understanding that the only way to experience that was to start in Hopkinton and run the whole way to Boston. And that was followed by a firm resolve to do this insane thing.

The Boston Marathon is a qualifiers-only race, and to qualify, a runner has to have a sub-2:30 time on some other marathon—OR—to be a sponsored charity runner—and that was my only hope. DFMC (the Dana-Farber Marathon Challenge team) has the best record of getting regular runners ready to finish the marathon. So, the next day I began hounding and harassing the DFMC offices. I was relentless, and after two weeks of talking and networking, I think they gave up. I was accepted to the team and now had to raise the obligatory $2,500 as a charity runner, which I felt was no problem for me, a natural enroller. The real problem was I couldn't run a mile and I was a big Clydesdale of a horse to boot. I recalled that the first marathoner, a big strong soldier, had dropped dead after running the distance from Marathon Plains to Athens to proclaim victory. And I didn't want to have a heart attack and die. I wanted to run the marathon.

DFMC was understanding and I began training the following week. One mile turned into three and three into six. I had a local six -mile run near my home that rounded a corner by the fire station and then ascended a pretty steep hill, which I fantasized to be my "heartbreak hill," the most difficult part of the Boston Marathon, that also began at a fire station on the corner of Commonwealth Avenue. Each run wasn't counted in terms of miles but in terms of the percentage of the marathon distance: 2.6 miles was 10 percent, 5.2 miles was just under 20 percent, and so on. I ate like a marathoner, I slept like a marathoner, and I set my calendar to the goals and numbers I needed to achieve so as not to die at the finish line. Everything I did was in terms of the marathon. Rigor takes the lead role in lining up everything in support of the objective.

The other thing that added rigor and which we previously referred to as the "activation energy" was that DFMC pairs their charity runners with some kid in treatment, so you have a vision of why you are really running. To this day I don't really know if my resolve would have pulled me across the finish line. But meeting Danny certainly did. On those days when it was cold and miserable outside, one thought of that bald-headed little kid, battling leukemia every moment of every day, made my discomfort seem small. Rigor, it turns out, needs a ton of reinforcement to stay immovable and unshakable. I became that rigorous. I became that determined. And the following April, I became a marathon runner. Race day came with me weighing in at 201 and fully capable of finishing the race. I didn't do a cartwheel, but the joy of seeing that blue and gold archway down the street by the public library is indescribable.

Rigor is an indispensable element of commitment. It forces all else around you to conform to the goal and vision. It creates the filter through which you see everything. But rigor is only half of the full equation. The other element is urgency. Urgency, like rigor, has a kind of bad reputation in most people's mind. We tend to think of things like medical emergencies, house fires, and the like. But adopting an urgency about your goals adds to the preemptive nature of the commitment. If in fact your house were on fire and your kids were on the second floor, there is no doubt in my mind that the urgency with which you strived to rescue them or pleaded with the firefighters to do that would be at a peak level.

So perhaps your house is not on fire! But we often jokingly refer to our state as "pants-on-fire urgency." The truth is that you do not need a fire to summon your urgency. Knowing that you *would* be that urgent and intense is enough. Knowing that it is already within your power and within your body means that it is already there. It is within your capacity and is one of your superpowers you inherited as a human being. You were born with it. So create a little urgency in your life. Let people know what your hairy, audacious goals are. Share your great vision publicly. Put yourself in a position where you must be urgent. Muhammad Ali was thought by many to be an egotistic braggart. But in actuality his making outrageous claims and predictions forced his hand. He now had to show up as the greatest, lest he would be thought of as a fool! He made those claims to force his own urgency in training.

Urgency is a way of being that makes anything that is not its priority, secondary. When we are urgent, *nothing* else matters. Urgency creates a single-minded state. The goal, the act, that which is your commitment is the only thing that drives you. Let's say you have a promise to deliver a project plan at work by Friday at 4 p.m. But doing so is dependent on three other departments getting their estimates to you beforehand—and none of them have delivered. Wednesday comes and you know that there is a lot of work yet to be done on the plan after you get those other departments' data. You become urgent. Remember, your urgency is yours alone and not theirs. Just because you feel urgent does not mean that they will.

Urgency does not whine. Urgency does not complain. Urgency is contagious, however. Because you have this single-mindedness, you bring a certain energy with you into the communications you have. Urgency does not use the telephone or email—it is direct, person-to-person, and unshakable. As soon as you notice that something is needed, you march over to your associate and begin the conversation, but because you are urgent, you don't waste any time on why something was not done or what got in the way. You are focused intently on what has to get done in order for you to get what you need. There is no room for circumstances (as we have already discussed), just a laser-like focus on completion. Urgency drives a focus on what, how, and by when. But you do not accept the normal "by when" fluff of "this is how long it normally takes." With urgency you drive toward the best, fastest, and most efficient time that serves your needs. Remember, your house is on fire. There are no other options than getting to that goal, now!

Scarcity and Abundance

Previously in this book we mentioned limiting beliefs and the feeling of scarcity. Scarcity is that feeling that there is never enough: not enough food, not enough money all which often flow from the thought that I am not enough (I don't have what it takes). Scarcity developed when we were quite young. We learn about 90 percent of our vocabulary before the age of five. All of your big, polysyllabic words represent only about 10 percent of your adult vocabulary. While we were learning all those words, we were also learning what those words described in the world—the meaning of the words. But while we were busy learning about our words and our world, we learned also that the world is bigger, faster, stronger, and smarter than we were as young toddlers and preschoolers. In other words, we learned that we were not big, fast, strong, and smart enough to keep up. This creates what psychologist Alfred Adler called an "inferiority complex."

As a result of learning this contrast of feeling little and small, we formed one of two reactions. We either thought, "Oh yeah, watch this!" or we thought, "Oh gee, I guess I really am a nothing." Maybe yours wasn't exactly phrased that way, but the bottom line is that we either set out to prove the big, fast, strong, smart world that we were good enough or we surrendered to the inferiority position. However, either case is still based in the feeling that we developed in those learning years that we were NOT (bigger, faster, stronger, and smarter). The place we start from—our "come from" as we like to all it—is that little child, less-than mentality. One way or the other, we all have that floating around somewhere inside.

When we come from a place of less-than, the world looks just like when we were little. Scarcity is a childlike mindset that fears things will be taken away. Three-year-old children go through the "mine" stage (as any parent can attest). Feeling that scarcity, the child starts labeling everything as "mine:"

- If I am playing with it, it is mine.

- If I was playing with it but am not now, it is still mine.

- If you are playing with it, but I want it, it is mine.

- If I haven't even thought about it before now and suddenly notice it across the room—you guessed it—it is mine!

Scarcity is hard-wired into our subconscious minds by the time we get to school. Then formal learning takes over and we seem to forget that scarcity is still the operating context running the show. We find ourselves competing for grades, to be the teacher's favorite, to belong to "the" group of favored kids, to be liked, to be picked on the team—the list goes on and on. Competing for the limited praise, resources, grades, and approval pits us alone against the rest of the world. And we never realize that what is driving it is our little child's thought pattern that we are just little and not enough on our own.

Abundance

The opposite of scarcity is abundance. Like scarcity, abundance is a mindset. Abundance is not the presence of lots of things, tons of money, and the satisfaction of our every desire. And like scarcity, abundance is a learned state. But scarcity and abundance live in an either/or duality. You cannot be kind of abundant and in scarcity. You either are owned by your substrate of scarcity or you have stepped fully into abundance. You just can't be both at the same time. So if you want to choose abundance, you will have to let go of your scarcity thoughts. Of course, we may not be able to stay totally in abundance at all times.

This may shock you, but nature does not have self-storage units. Nowhere in nature does hoarding exist. Only humans hoard things. Only humans seem to think that more is better and that they actually "need" more than they have. That is a direct result of the scarcity mindset. Advertising plays on our scarcity mindset by telling us we really do need this next new product. We have bumper stickers that say things like "The winner is the one who dies with the most toys." But nature does quite well without hoarding. Things in nature, even higher level animals, even squirrels, take only what they need. Nature lives in abundance—there is enough for everyone. The realities of the world and life can and will slap us around from time to time. And when it does, we may slip back into our old scarcity thinking. So let's look into how we can learn an abundant mindset and what it takes to re-center ourselves in abundance when we slip off.

Abundance mindset starts with gratitude. Instead of looking for what is missing, we begin with what we have already. You will never draw more toward you if you are looking for what is missing. Conversely, when you already are grateful for what you have, you suddenly become aware of more than you already have. Gratitude is a practice—and practiced daily. And gratitude is perhaps the single most consistently taught principle of every great teacher and sage in human history. It is not possible that they are all wrong or fooled by some universal trickster! So, before we can talk about building abundance, we develop a practice of gratitude—an attitude of gratitude, if you will!

Start each day by writing down five things for which you are genuinely grateful. At first you will be tempted to list things (stuff you have) like a house or roof over your head, friends, and family. But we would like to suggest that you start by listing the really big things: your life (you woke up today—hallelujah!), your breath, your mind, your health, your body. Start with the fundamentals and then work up to the other things. It is important to write these in your journal or a notebook because the act of writing means that you are tripling the effect of your being grateful: First you think the thought, then you write it down (a second time of thought), and thirdly you see the written gratitude, furthering its awareness in your mind. In fact, stop reading right now and list five to ten things you are grateful for.

Starting your day is just half of the discipline of gratitude. The other is building a nightly routine of being thankful for the day (oh look, I survived another day!). Seriously, ending your day with a gratitude list, recalling some of the wonderful and not-so-wonderful-but-learning experiences of the day, will double down the power of gratitude. Do each of them daily for at least twenty-one days to build the habit and watch what happens. In order to build that daily routine, place a pad or a journal on your nightstand and post reminders around the house to help remember (nothing beats a sticky note on the bathroom mirror saying "Did I write my gratitude list?"). The bottom line of practicing gratitude is that you cannot prepare yourself to receive abundance until you are grateful for what you have received already.

Abundance is the natural state of the universe. There are more stars than we can count, more galaxies than we can conceive of, and here on old planet Earth, there are more resources, more elements and more of anything we could want than we are capable of conceiving. Furthermore, as we mentioned early on in this text, you are composed of the same matter as the stars and the universe, and therefore you are a part of the infinite abundance of all things. It literally is who you are. The bottom line is our minds are relatively finite in their imagination in contrast to the abundance of what surrounds us. So why do we not see all of the abundance? It is actually a matter of biology and psychology.

Inside your brain is a small part referred to as the Reticular Activating Formation. It is part of our most primitive or reptilian brain. Its function, called the reticular activating system or RAS for short, was developed through evolution as a survival mechanism. Its job is to separate foreground (what is deemed as important) from background (the lesser important things). The brain is continually bombarded by zillions of stimuli from all of our sensory systems and frankly we would go mad were it not for the sorting system of the RAS. So essentially what happens is that over time the brain learns what is important to focus on and what is not, what is essential for surviving and what is not. By shifting the stimuli of lesser importance to background noise, we are able to drive a car, have a prolonged conversation, or do our homework without derailment.

So, when we talk about the abundance of all of those desired things already surrounding you, thank your RAS for the fact that you just don't focus on them and therefore think that they don't exist. Think of the new car phenomenon. Let's imagine that you decide to buy a new car and instead of just getting an upgrade of your current vehicle, you go shopping. The salesperson walks you around the lot interviewing you for your likes and needs and introduces you to a vehicle you have never seen or noticed before. But because your salesperson has done a great job, it is an ideal fit. You take it for a test drive, kick the tires as it were, and decide that day to buy it. But here comes the RAS. On the way home you suddenly see not only ten cars of that make and model, but ten of the exact same color, make, and model! It seems as though while you were out buying your car, a whole heap of other people decided to buy the same car because you have never seen or heard of this one before and suddenly they are everywhere!

Wrong!

They were already everywhere, but the RAS had deemed them unimportant for survival and paid no attention to them. But now that you have one, its importance has been elevated and you suddenly see that which was there the entire time.

A person we know, we'll call him Fred, married a woman who was a pure dynamo of finance. She was a former CFO of a large banking firm and had left that role to start her own financial management and consulting firm. Fred loved everything about her, but most of all he loved the silly quirk that she had. It seemed that everywhere they went Suze stopped along the way to pick up loose change on their path, a penny here or a nickel and sometimes a dollar—once a twenty-dollar bill! Suze operated with a belief that the world was an abundant source of wealth. Fred on the other hand, being a frugal man, believed that if anyone would have dropped their money, they would either pick it up or, upon discovering it to be missing, would retrace their steps to find it. This resulted in his belief that there is no money lying around. During the time of their courtship, Fred started counting what Suze found, and by the time he proposed marriage to her, he had counted over four hundred and thirty dollars that she had collected on their dates. So impressed was he by this curious habit that his proposal was sitting on her desk at the end of a long trail of some fifty dollars of quarters he had set out on a path for her to find! It seems that abundance is in the eye of the beholder.

And that is precisely our point: We need to train our eyes and our minds to see the abundance. It is not something that we can conjure up. Rather, abundance exists—all the time, everywhere. And just because you cannot see it, this does not prove that it does not exist. It only supports the hypothesis that your RAS has not been trained and that your belief system holds on to the stubborn belief that there is not enough of whatever you are seeking to go around. So while gratitude is the first step in realizing abundance, the second step is to train your mind. One of the most effective methods of mental training is the use of affirmations. Below is a list of affirmations that have to do with abundance, and we invite you to create your own "abundance list." We have listed some ideas to start you off below, but don't stop with our list. Generate more.

- I am the source of my abundance; I will see it everywhere I look.

- I trust that the infinite universe is naturally and totally abundant.

- There is no limit to what I can create when I let abundance flow through me.

- I am becoming a master at creating whatever I want.

- I am linking with the unlimited abundance of my higher self.

- I am opening my connection to the higher forces (God, Source).

- I live each day in gratitude.

- I start each day with a gratitude list and end the night being thankful.

- I am expanding my beliefs about what I deserve to have.

- I focus on what I want and draw it to me.

- I am grateful for all that surrounds me.

- The more I evolve, the more power my thoughts have to create my reality.

- I have unlimited abundance.

- I live in an abundant world and all is perfect in the universe.

- I create my prosperity no matter what the economy is like.

- I can have a wonderful, positive, and abundant life.

- My choices and possibilities are expanding every day.

- I am always thinking in bigger and unlimited ways.

- My unlimited thinking increases my creativity.

- My unlimited thinking expands my possibilities.

- My unlimited thinking draws opportunities to me.

- My unlimited thinking helps me get in touch with the bigger picture of my life.

- My unlimited thinking links me with the greater vision of my higher self.

- My unlimited thinking helps me fulfill my potential.

- I unfold my potential by imagining my dreams coming true.

- My dreams and fantasies are guiding me to a higher path on earth.

- I love and trust my imagination.

- My imagination helps me to transcend my physical world.

- My imagination gives me the ability to step outside of my personal limits.

- My imagination creates unlimited future pathways for me.

- I am an unlimited being and can create anything I want.

- My clear intention generates energy that goes out and gets what I want.

- I allow all of my dreams to come true.

Using affirmations like these is not a practice of naïve optimism. It is a matter of training your mind to be able to see what is already there. Like doing a gratitude list (which also activates the RAS to start looking for things for which we are grateful), building a set of positive affirmations around abundance activates the RAS to see abundance. We will say a bit more about being optimistic and having positive intentions in the final section of this book.

The third practice of abundance is giving. Now this might sound counterintuitive. How can I give something away when I feel like I am in scarcity? Precisely! You can't. In fact, in order to give something away you are forced to see what you have. While we are writing this book, the world is gripped in the throes of a pandemic. Well before the forced shutdowns, I lost all of my second and third quarter contracts. Companies were already choosing not to have corporate travel or to allow outside consultants in the building. Then they stopped having all group gatherings. The net result was that I was facing at least the next three quarters with absolutely no income in sight. I suddenly felt that there was not going to be enough money to make it.

Then the lockdown came, and the fear became certainty! So, in a moment of determination, I went to the local grocery store (with gloves and mask on, of course) and went directly to the bank kiosk where I withdrew one hundred dollars in ten-dollar bills. I went to each of the cashiers and four stockers and handed each one a ten, and said, "I am so grateful that you are here doing this right now. Thank you!" By the time I got to my car I was feeling so abundant, so joyful and so grateful that I was both grinning and welled up with tears of joy. It was incredibly freeing. Though I could have done the same thing with ten or fifty dollars, a hundred was a bigger stretch and, frankly, the thought of doing it scared me. But the breakthrough on the other side was worth the price.

When you give of yourself, whether monetarily or through your talents, you are forced into a mindset that recognizes what you have and what your gifts are. There is no other way to do it. But here is the thing: When you travel to third world locations and meet with people who on our scale of economy have nothing to speak of, you will find them to be among the most giving and abundant people you will ever meet. They know that their survival as a group depends on their mutual sharing and giving. So it becomes a way of life to give. To us as outsiders, it seems illogical, but to those in this village it is a fact of life.

Giving cannot be done with any intent to receive (either a thank you or something of equal value in return). Giving by definition is unconditional. It has no strings attached nor expectations of anything in return. It is a pure act of giving. Abundance is given to another with absolutely no expectations or requirements. Because you were born into this life, you are an inheritor of this universe's abundance. In the knowledge of that gift, we get to give, and by giving, we notice our own abundance. Practice gratitude, affirmations to train the brain and unconditional giving, and you will unlock the power of the universe's abundance. You will become a source of abundance for yourself.

And finally, the remaining practice in abundance is belief. It is essential that you believe that the nature of the universe and of life in general is abundance. That means you, as part of the universe, are also abundant and abundantly creative. One way to test your belief in abundance is around your intention setting. Your intention is related to your goal or your vision. You see something that is your future desire and you set an intention to get there. Your intention will cause you to start doing things to move in the direction of your vision. Your rigor and urgency is your part. As we discussed under that section, your rigor and urgency gets you prepared and ensures that you put in the work required. When you bring your full intention to the starting line, you have done your part.

But, trusting in the abundance of the universe, you then must let go of any attachment to how it looks or what the actual results will be. If you do not let go of being attached (knowing or thinking you know) to what the outcomes should be, you will limit the results to just those that you alone can produce. Let us assure you that the universe is far more powerful and far more abundant than your imagination. So not trusting in that abundance limits all the other possible outcomes that might be the result of your goal and intention.

My friend Sky left the East Coast because she felt called to the lifestyle of Southern California. A single woman, she felt that she might have a better shot at meeting the kind of health-conscious man she desired by living there—not to mention expanding her mission to serve others while creating more income and time flexibility in her own life. So she took a leap of faith. Sky set about starting her business and did fairly well but she also began looking for dates and mature, accomplished potential life partners through dating services and social media.

While her business flourished, her dating didn't. On a visit to her place in California, Sarah and I sat with her, expanding her vision of a life together with her ideal. After completing the exercise, I suggested letting go and trusting the universe. We crumpled up the vision chart and threw it away. Wait for it—within just a few months, Deris walked into one of her presentations. He was smart, handsome, and an accomplished inventor and businessman, and it didn't take long for them to connect. Two years later, Sky and Deris were married and the following year they had purchased their house. But the rest of the story is that Sky is now the top producer in her company and is enjoying a life beyond her dreams with a compassionate man who cherishes her and supports her in every way. Her rigorous hard work certainly paid off but so too did her letting go of how it should look.

The Power behind Source – Self-Awareness

Urgency, rigor and abundance are just three of the more important elements of source. Self-awareness—a clear and healthy self-awareness—is the most important foundation. So far in this book we have discussed how the false self (or ego) forms our self-concept and how those concepts are built over a lifetime of interactions, actions and results. But a healthy self-awareness, which is the foundation of our ability to be that source of our lives, is a clear understanding of that mature self. Who we are, who we intend to be, the results and feedback that allow us to modify our behaviors, and an awareness of our part in the grand scheme of the universe are all aspects of total self-awareness.

In working with and coaching high performers in the corporate world, one of the key characteristics of a high performer is the accuracy of her self-awareness. High performers know their strengths and weaknesses and know how to play to their strengths and how to compensate for their lesser skills. Conversely, one of the indicators of poorer performance is a lack of self-awareness or an inaccurate sense of one's skills. Living as the source and sole author of your future is a life of high performance and requires an accurate level of self-awareness.

Self-awareness allows you to differentiate between you and your results, between feedback and other people's opinions, and know the difference between what your ego wants to believe and your accurate assessment of your skills. Self-awareness is the result of a hunger for feedback and a practice of A/B testing. People who are self-aware not only take in the feedback, they alter their actions and then seek further feedback on whether that course correction worked or not. Self-awareness comes with a measure of humility behind it—there is no room for ego and its tendency to overrate your abilities. And the bottom line of self-awareness is that it is a process of continually seeking to better oneself.

And while we are talking about skills and abilities, there is one more piece of self-awareness we get to discuss. Every skill can be taken to an extreme where it creates a toxic side effect. It is inaccurate to say that a skill can become a weakness—because a skill is always a skill. But they can produce a negative and sometimes career- or relationship-limiting side effect. For example, we all know a super smart person who is a bit over the top and becomes arrogant and abrasive. They are no less intelligent, but their intellect is so turbo-charged without a balance of empathy or self-awareness that it makes others feel "less than" and often becomes an interruptive force.

The same is true for any skill. Who wouldn't want the best, most customer-oriented person on their sales team? But taken to the extreme, customer service can overpromise to the client and then beat up the home team for not meeting those expectations, or for being compelled to offer deep discounts that erode all profit. The "thrill of the hunt" can overshadow offering the best possible product or service. Or take ethics as an example: we all want to operate from a strong set of ethics, but taken to the extreme, ethics become moralistic and rigid, making everyone else wrong.

Self-awareness requires noticing the unintended effects of our overused skills and seeks to find the balancing or compensating skills. If you are an action junkie and perhaps use that to the extreme, your quick trigger and penchant for action can be balanced by engaging others in the decision process. That way everyone is running at the same pace. There is a great book on this subject called *FYI: For Your Improvement*[18] that identifies some sixty to seventy key leadership skills, what they look like as overused or underdeveloped skills, what would compensate for overuse of the skill, and how to strengthen it, if it is in need of development.

In my job for the year before my maternity leave, I was the top producer of sales. So much so that one colleague said he felt like they were all stuck on a freeway traffic jam and I took the emergency exit. I shot back at him that I actually felt like I was on that freeway and dragging all the other cars along with me as well as having a parachute slowing me down! But I took that "emergency exit," and during my maternity leave none of the deals I had in my pipeline came through. It was so concerning that I feared losing my job. So, when I returned to work, I went directly to the CFO and said that I didn't think I should be retained as none of my deals produced revenue, and that I had failed in bringing my colleagues along in the process so that they could close them (I actually had overused my skill of individual performance). His response was that because of that self-awareness, I was retained and, in fact, ended up getting a raise and promotion so that I could better lead the others.

Sourcing Your Future – An Exercise In Visioning

As you are reaching an understanding of how you have sourced your past or present, you may be asking yourself, "How do I use this knowledge to source my future?" We have a fun exercise to get you started. We call it a "letter of accomplishment"—write a letter to yourself from the future self (a year from now) congratulating yourself for what you had accomplished in the year and what it took for you to accomplish it. Now expand that list to include each area of your life that will be important to you in the coming year: your fitness, your relationships, places that you have traveled,

18 Michael Lombardo and Robert Eichinger. *FYI: For Your Improvement – A Guide for Development and Coaching* (Minneapolis, MN: Lominger Limited, Inc., 2004).

career, finances, and social or community involvement. You can find a great description of the letter of accomplishment in *The Art of Possibility* by Rosamund and Benjamin Zander.[19] Give yourself an A in the class of life and tell yourself, in detail, what you had to do to get that A.

That was the warm-up exercise.

Now, in your journal, create a section called your "Dream List," a tool designed by Matthew Kelly, author of *The Dream Manager*. You can make it as long as you like and can include as many different areas of your life as you wish. It could be in the realm of finance, career, profession, physical health, family, intimacy, spirituality, interests, or travel—you decide—but leave space between each category down the page(s) and try to get at least ten categories. Across the top of the (each) page list *six months to one year, five years,* and in your *lifetime*. It doesn't matter what categories you choose. What matters is that it is a list of your biggest dreams, hopes, and ambitions. Then in each bucket (six months, five years, life), list three to five specific dreams you have for that category. So you will eventually end up with upwards of fifteen dreams for each of your ten categories.

Most people will run dry somewhere between fifty to seventy dreams. When you've reached this point, share your list with a close friend, lover, parent, or family member who really knows you well, asking them to add any dreams that you have talked about in the past, things you might have forgotten, or dreams that you have since become jaded about. Once you have gotten a full and complete list of your dreams, review the entire list and highlight at least *one dream* in each category that is your highest desire in that area. It is also helpful to notice what themes you see in each category that relate to your highest desire. Additionally, out of those highlighted dreams and the general themes, what is the one overarching theme of your Dream List—your truest desire for each of the categories all rolled into one. This will point you to what your true desire is for your life—your true north star—and should help add further clarity to the highest desire in each of your categories. Perhaps add your "why" after each dream.

The final step is to pick someone to be your accountability partner for each of your truest desires. This is the person who is most likely to support

19 Benjamin Zander and Rosamund Stone Zander, *The Art of Possibility: Transforming Professional and Personal Life.* (New York: Penguin Group, 2000).

you in accomplishing your dream. Share your dream with them and a date by when you will have accomplished it. This is a person who will keep checking with you, asking your intentions, what you are doing about your dream, because you said it was the most important, and they will not let you fail.

Kris Girrell & Candace Sjogren

–**6**–

Shifting to Source

Stages and States

Transformation is a process with no particular end. It is not a place you ever "get to" and, in fact, it is not even a process that you "get"— as in you thoroughly understand how it works. Often, we are fond of saying that there is nothing to get until you get it that there is nothing to get. We see this in many of the transformation programs that we run. Many of our students are smart enough to thoroughly understand what is going on, but their habits and ego will not yet allow them to surrender to the process, and so, while they may talk the talk, they don't yet walk the talk. They continue to recreate their frustrating circumstances, unwilling to acknowledge that they, in fact, are the source.

Philosopher Ken Wilbur makes an important distinction between what he calls stages and states.

- **Stages** are your outward way of being – it is essentially your vocalized thought based on a conscious understanding of the complexity of things. Stage is not simply a mental/egoist knowing. It might be like knowing an acrobatic routine, a dance move or a martial arts Kata.

You may know all the moves long before you are accomplished at doing the routine. Your Stage is simply your knowledge of the dance, without having acted it out. More recently Wilbur has been referring to this as "waking up."

- Your **state** is your inner awareness or your inner aliveness or functioning – how you "be." Your state is a state of being that is exposed by how you show up in the world and can only be seen by the reflective mirror of feedback. Your State pulls you forward into being and is generally a step or two ahead of your functional Stage. Similarly, Ken has more recently been referring to this element as "growing up."

While we can think of stages and states as separate or discrete steps, in fact they are more like two parallel tracks on a continuum. So it is possible to have awakened to the various levels of understanding but to have not yet grown up into that practiced way of being. You really have to both wake up and grow up.

Wilbur describes the process as one of "transcend and include" meaning that each time we evolve to a next level of being we may move past our old ways and habits, but parts of them are always retained. For example, in our basic ways of being we think of things as black/white, good/bad certainties that psychology calls "dualistic." Things are either good or bad. But as we grow, we come to learn about ways of being that are "both/and." Living from both/and does not mean that there are no longer absolutes—those can still exist (e.g., murder is still "bad"). But in our higher state of functioning, we prefer to come mostly from that inclusive state of both/and.

In development, as in transformation, the goal is to be congruent between your inner and outer being, between your Stage and your State—or waking up and growing up. But often those don't coincide. You can be aware of the levels and processes of human transformation and be able to describe what a highly evolved state looks like and acts like but be speaking into that from a place (Stage) of individualism or egoism, even arrogance. You can talk quite knowledgeably about psychology, theology, spirituality, emotional intelligence, and transformation and yet not have experienced those transitions you may easily be able to describe. Think of an example of someone who has exhibited this in your life. They are often easy to spot from the outside. On the other hand, you could be highly evolved and come from a high state of unitive consciousness and yet have little knowledge of the process or the theories that describe it. Some of the wisest gurus were simple people with no education to speak of at all (though I believe that Ken Wilbur would contend that they would be both away and grown up). Incongruence is simply the size of the gap between your awareness and your behavior— between your waking up and your growing up.

Heather is a part-time talk show host and a real champion of positivity on the Internet. Her over twelve thousand followers love her posts that encourage positive thinking and committed action. She has a sultry and infectious laugh and is a practitioner of what she calls "Laughter Yoga." But inside Heather is alone and lonely. She can't hold a steady job, her talk show is on and off the air, and she survives by house-sitting around the world (not bad, as you view it from the outside, but it earns no money for her), resulting in what she calls her "nomadic lifestyle." Her "job" and lifestyle keep her detached and alone, never staying in any place long enough to put down roots and build a support community. Heather has no savings, no income, and really no future she can hope for. When we talk to Heather, she knows exactly what we are talking about and she sets a strong intention. The only problem is that she does not believe it, nor does she believe enough in herself to be able to "pull it off," as she calls it. When we point out that the idea of "pulling it off" is an ego-driven thought that has no space for the power of the universe to be engaged, she will resist or defend a bit and then say, rather dejectedly, "yeah, I know." Stage-wise, Heather gets it. State-wise she is still in the starting blocks and has been stuck there for decades.

Grant is another example. Grant is highly successful as a businessman and consultant, running several businesses, all of which are profitable. Grant uses transformational language in his practice of consulting and coaching business leaders. He is married to a lovely wife who herself is a successful leader in her field, and they live comfortably in a tastefully appointed house outside the city. By all outward appearances, Grant is the dead opposite of Heather: successful, a leader, and apparently happy and well-adjusted. But in encountering Grant, one gets the feeling that there is something not quite congruent—the words and the music don't seem to match. While he is a take-charge leader, a lot of that comes from his ego and the need to be recognized as the leader, the consultant, the guru. There is something that taints his communications that feels like it is all about him—there is a lot more of "I" and "me" than there is of "us" and "we." And yet, when push comes to shove, he does apply many of the teachings of this "technology" quite effectively. He is an example of high-level stage awareness but with a state of development lagging more than a couple steps behind in terms of growing up.

In law school the saying goes that *A* students become judges, *B* students become law professors (because they tend to focus on stages not states) and the *C* students most often become practicing lawyers, because their focus is all about the state not the stages.

The Practices of Source

Understanding stages and states is itself a stage-related idea. But becoming aware of the differences between where you think you are in stage and where you actually "be" as your state is a powerful distinction that can radically improve your transformational development. The stage is usually slightly ahead of the state (at least one step ahead) so you have an idea of what it would look like to be functioning at that next state. Telling yourself the truth about your stage and state difference will keep you moving forward toward your goal. We call this "plus-oneing" yourself. Fully learning the intricacies and behaviors of the stage one step in front of your currently functional state is like dangling a carrot in front of yourself. Just keep clear that knowing about it is not being it (at least not yet).

Here are a few practices that may be helpful in becoming more congruent with your stage and state:

Feedback

Your number one tool that we learn and practice in all elements of our transformation training at BBA is giving and getting effective feedback. Feedback (not opinion) when treated as "just information" can help you discern how your actions are showing up to others. The important element of getting effective feedback is asking effective questions. Experiment with how to ask the question. For example, just asking, "How am I showing up?" is too general and will not provide any practicable information. Conversely, saying, "I am working on not coming from ego and coming instead from a place of 'I'm enough'" might give the other person too many clues about what you are hoping to hear from her. Practice asking for feedback multiple ways until you find a few questions that work well for you. One tip, though, is to be certain to ask the people offering you feedback "what is missing?" It is a really good way to get actionable information. In this example, simply "I have received feedback that I operate from ego. As you experience me, what is missing from me in order to overcome this?"

Declarations and Intentions

Since your state most often lags behind your stage, you might make a practice of declaring a state-based intention. The process of declaring it aloud, to others who are important to you, puts your behaviors in motion. Despite having a relatively big gap between your awareness and your actions, the goal is always trending toward closing the stage/state gap. Start by envisioning what it might be like to operate from a lack of ego, or always coming from compassion or any of the elements of a higher state of evolution. Then declare a day (or week or just an hour if that is all you can do) of acting "as if" you are functioning at that level. Practice makes perfect, as they say. For instance, "Starting today, I will become known for my humility."

Defragging

The advanced part of integrating our state with our stage is understanding that we tend to compartmentalize actions. I often talk to people about being three-dimensional, a term I use to describe some of the great masters:

1. They are a serious force to be reckoned with.

2. They exude tolerance and acceptance.

3. They never take themselves so seriously that they can't laugh at themselves.

The masters (think of HH the Dalai Lama) seem to embody all three states simultaneously while we often toggle from light-hearted to compassionate to that serious force of nature. Defragging (or defragmenting) is working to make the blend as seamless and simultaneous as possible.

Related, but not synonymous to your state of being is your physical state: turned on, tuned in, nervous, jazzed, sluggish, determined, and so on. The general rule about your physical and emotional being is that you cannot occupy two places at the same time. That is, you cannot be happy and sad at the same time; you cannot be sluggish and excited at the same time; or sleepy and wide awake at the same time. The field of Neuro-Linguistic Programming (or NLP for short) informs us that your body and your central nervous system (and by extension, your emotional state) are "hard-wired" together. What affects one affects the other. Try it: look up at the ceiling with a big grin on your face and try to think of some depressive thought. You can't. The physiology of depression is frowning and head bowed down.

We have learned a cool trick over the years: You can use your physical being to change your mental/emotional state of being. If you are feeling nervous or out of sorts, stand up, put your shoulders back, smile, and do a giant fist-pump "YES!" Most likely the hair on the back of your neck will stand up, you will get goose bumps all over and suddenly feel much more energized. It has been proven time and time again that you can shift your state—physical or emotional—any time you choose. But you have to make the choice. Simply saying, "I choose to be excited and happy" is not sufficient sometimes. It often takes a physical action to shift your physical/emotional being.

Your Default Context

Everyone operates automatically from a contextual frame. Essentially, you have a default context—that is, the sense-making inside your mind is comprised of everything you have ever learned, experienced, or were socialized to know. It lives deep inside the brain and is used as a filter. When we learn something new, it is compared to what we already know. This is a process called "associative learning." And those concepts, memories, and experiences form what we call "context." Think of this like how you better understand what is happening in a picture when you know the context in which the picture was taken. Context provides a framing or a meaning. You do in fact have an ongoing, ever-present context. The leaders at Landmark Education have a phrase for this called your "already/always" way of

Typhoon Honey

listening—you already have a meaning you use and you are always applying that meaning-making structure to everything.

Similar to your default context or your already/always way of listening is something called your implicit bias. Harvard has a website[20] where you can test your implicit bias over fifteen different assessments. By analyzing your speed and reactions to differing scenarios, you will get an assessment of how biased you are toward things like race, gender, age, weight and so on. It is well worth the few minutes each test takes to see where you actually score.

Your default context is already there and always will be. However, the wonderful thing about being Homo sapiens is that we can think about our thought process. In other words, knowing that we have a context, and having a sense of that context, we can supplant the default context with a temporary context. We know that we will eventually snap back to our default context until we have new meaning making (which is the purpose of transformation, after all), but we can create this new context for this single event.

Changing Your Context – Creating CPR

Perhaps you are familiar with the popular notion of starting with your *why*, as preached by motivational speaker Simon Sinek.[21] Essentially the idea is that we are all more motivated when we have a strong reason why we are doing what we are doing. Creating a new context is a process of identifying and solidifying your why. We would like to introduce a concept called CPR. A CPR (which stands for Context, Purpose, and Results) is an exercise/ document structure that anyone can use individually or as a group to create a clear picture of "why" in a way that stays in the forefront of any activity while it's being done.

A CPR can be done for any activity, from a meeting or a project to having that heart-to-heart conversation with a loved one. They can be done by individuals, couples, and teams. It's quite flexible and works well when you want to create something that didn't exist before or to give more structure and purpose to your vision. We call it a CPR because like cardiopulmonary

---

20 Project Implicit, Harvard University, https://implicit.harvard.edu/implicit/takeatest.html
21 Simon Sinek, *Start with Why: How Great Leaders Inspire Everyone.* (New York: Penguin Group, 2011).

151

resuscitation, it breathes new life into your process, project, or conversation. However, creating a CPR starts with the R—your results.

Defining your results is like standing in the future, at the moment of completion of this activity and looking around at all the outcomes you created. We sometimes refer to them as "finally" results—like "I am finally clear of all debt," or "we finally have the open communication our marriage deserves." What are all the results or outcomes you want to see when this is done? Outcomes should be specific, measurable results like having completed writing this document, or observable like we were all on the same page and in agreement.

Your results can be anything, really, but the key in writing good results is that they are written as if they have already happened (as in past tense—like "we completed X") and that they be written as a positive action (as in what was done as opposed to what was not done — you can't observe was something was not done just because you haven't seen it yet). Your results have to be something that you can observe and know is a completed outcome. For most projects and short-term issues, we suggest no more than four to six outcomes or results. If you or your team are working on a larger and longer-term project, you may wish to have more outcomes/results. But keep them manageable, observable, and concrete. With your results clear, you can then move to creating the Purpose line.

A purpose statement is your clear statement of intention (something we will get to in a few pages). Essentially your purpose is to create those results, so a quick way of creating a first pass at your purpose statement is to say "to cause X, Y, and Z (your results) to happen." But it is better if you refine your purpose line to be more easily read and committed to memory, because the purpose is the real "why" of this project.

Let's say that my results for a holiday with my family are the following:

- We had a wonderful and joy-filled holiday dinner.

- The table was a beautiful showcase of abundance.

- Everything was cooked to perfection.

- The entire family, to a person, asked when we could do it again.

Then my purpose simply stated might be "to create a dinner party where everything was so wonderful that we wanted to do it again." Or another person might create the purpose line to "host a dinner that brings us closer and celebrates the best of what we are as a family." The true test of a good purpose line is that reading it conjures up the completed results. So read the purpose and read a result—then ask yourself if you see that result coming from the purpose? Repeat that with each outcome.

If you are satisfied with your "why" or purpose statement, you are ready to create a context. This is the magical part of the process. A context is a brief phrase or image that represents the vision of what will be created. As a visual person, you might want to create a picture for the context. For example: Imagine your picture of how smoothly water flows over a rock in a river as a visual context for dealing with a difficult conversation. Or you might be more verbal, so your context could be like the Staples button, "That was easy!" In fact, the whole campaign for Staples was creating a context for people buying and using their products.

So let's go back to the dinner party. If my purpose was to create a dinner party where everything was so wonderful that we wanted to do it again, then what context would hold me to that purpose? I might choose one of "Food and family equals fun" or perhaps "we keep coming back for more." Whatever it is, your context needs to be something that when you read and follow it with one of your results, you can see how that context would help produce the result:

C: Keep coming back for more; R: wonderful, joy-filled dinner
C: Keep coming back for more; R: the table was a showcase of abundance
C: Keep coming back for more; R: everything cooked to perfection
C: Keep coming back for more; R: everyone asked when we could do it again

A context well written will keep you on track. It is like a centerline snapped down the floor, or like a little angel sitting on your shoulder that keeps reminding you to stay on purpose. The context should be easy to say, see, or remember and, like the results, easy to relate to the purpose. Your purpose should be evident by your context, image, or phrase. The process of writing a CPR helps generate a clear picture of the future (the Results) and gives an easy way (the Context) to be reminded of the "why" (the Purpose) of doing something while doing it.

Positive Intention And Grounded Optimism

When we discussed abundance, we mentioned that your intention has to be in partnership with the universe's nature of abundance which we call grounded optimism. Remember that the universe is an equal opportunity source of abundance. You cannot create an intention that results in your having something that would result in others not having. Abundance does not work like that. Abundance means enough for all. So setting a positive intention translates to setting an intention that results in all of us "winning" and all of us getting what we need. You cannot hope for abundance to show up in your life in a way that you get to keep it all to the exclusion of others. Abundance is for all and it must be free not only to flow into you but to flow through you and into others. Put another way, you trust in abundance, your vision and intention are based in that faith, but the abundance you receive is something that you get to share in service to others. When setting your intention, always ask yourself how this result can serve others.

I had an intention to buy out my business partner, but when I approached him, I found not only that the price was well above what I could afford, he actually wanted to do the deal a lot sooner than I had planned. I didn't know where I could come up with that kind of cash. But I reevaluated my business plan. My intention wasn't just to buy out my partner. What I really wanted to do was create a shared ownership where everyone could become an owner and grow with this business. When I settled into that vision, I felt a bit more relaxed but still had the challenge of coming up with cash. That is until my phone started ringing. It was my good friend from the West Coast. "you know how you've been talking about building a business with many partners?" she said (without prompting, I might add), "Well I want to invest in that."

Then there was another call and another. And in less than forty-eight hours I had every bit of funding needed for the deal. I gathered my new partners together and asked how we might create a valuation for this business (after all, training has no asset or capital equipment that could ever be liquidated). We could either set the value at the price of the deal or create one that we felt the business would be worth. I let go of any idea of what I thought it should be. These partners—who had just come together over the last two days—all agreed that they would value the business at the higher number in recognition of my work getting it all started!

Positive intention goes beyond doing no harm to others. It means that you set an intention for the good of all. An intention to become wealthy might be okay if your intention is to be wealthy enough to help others out of their poverty or wealthy enough to employ others who are struggling. If your intention is to have a big home, you might want to alter that to include others having room in that house. When Sarah and I wanted to buy a house, we set the intention of having a house big enough to have guests, so that we could help out people who needed housing, but we also held an intention that it be one that was ridiculously below the going market rate. Our goal was to get this house, on an acre of land, in a prime community where the going price at that time was between $500,000 and $600,000! Now houses in the area are more like three-quarters of a million dollars, but we wanted it at a cost that was below the current jumbo loan rate of $275,000.

Realtors told us that we were crazy and that it was impossible, but that did not deter us from looking and trusting that within the abundance of everything, such a bargain was available, especially because of our positive intention of serving others. In less than seven months we not only sold Sarah's house in Long Island (a financial prerequisite of this purchase), but we closed on a house at $270,000, in the best school district of one of the most sought-after communities in the state. To this day we have sheltered five people for as long as two years each and have recently turned the guest quarters into a low cost Airbnb suite that now makes money which we use for renovations. Positive intention produces positive results.

Continual Shifting – Surfing The Waves

Applying this principle to your intention results in being able to roll with the changes in your results as the universe provides new options. When you have a rigid set of outcomes that you expect as a result of your intention, anything the abundant universe sends your way will land on you as not what you intended and therefore will be denied or rejected by your willful mind. In a sense your strong intention about how the outcome should look is a limiting bottleneck on the flow of abundance.

But when we let go of how it has to look, we get to go surfing. Think of being a surfer. You paddle out into the rolling ocean knowing the conditions are just right that day for a great ride. As you sit on your board far out from shore, you watch the swells rise and fall as they come toward you. Then you see one with promise and you turn to face the shore and start paddling. Sometimes that swell is a great wave and sometimes it doesn't turn out to be much. But you are there to surf, so after each ride you paddle back out to your spot and await what the earth has to offer.

Shifting is like surfing. You don't get angry at the smaller swells that don't turn into big waves or spectacular rides. You trust that what is coming at you will include great rides and at the end of the day are delighted to have been out there communing with mother earth and what she provided that day. In fact, we never met a surfer who didn't say "any day of surfing is a good day!"

Shifting rolls with the waves and takes each new opportunity that is provided. With your vision and intention set on your future (somewhat like catching the big kahuna), you act based on the next right thing to do given what shows up in front of you. You trust implicitly in the universe and stay firmly grounded in your vision to guide you in "surfing" the changes and opportunities that the universe, in her infinite wisdom, will provide.

Kicked to the Curb

Standing as source is not always sunshine and roses. You may feel like you have this all handled when suddenly, out of the blue, life kicks you to the curb. It is not a bad thing or a good thing; it just is what happens sometimes in living life on life's terms. We often jokingly say, "Life is life-ing me today." That does not mean that you have not been source in your life. It means that life, the universe and everything (to borrow Douglas Adams's phrase) is chaos. And chaos is non-discriminatory. You are not exempt because you have chosen to live this life of source. And sometimes the randomness of the universe is not your feedback—but by now you know enough about feedback to tell which is yours and which is life just showing us as random chaos.

When life kicks you and you feel like you are down for the count, what can you do? First you accept and embrace the reality within those circumstances. Certainly, we have legitimate emotions as part of our being human and those emotions at times seem to whip us around. But it helps to differentiate the reaction to the event from the interpretation of that event that may have a tendency to produce a more intense emotional reaction that would normally be expected in the situation. So our first step is always to look at the event in and of itself—without evaluation or emotions. Then inspect your story. Take a good look at the evaluations or interpretations you are making about this situation. Start with the emotions you are feeling and then unpackage them. We use a method called the "ABCD method" and it has four steps:

- **A** (step one) The A stands for the **Actual** and factual event. What, really, is happening —no story about it, no evaluations ("this is so terrible" or "impossible"); just what has happened or is happening, right now? Try to get a clear perspective without evaluation by asking several friends and associates (especially those who are also on this path) what they see as actuality.

- B (There is something that happens between A and C, but we'll come back to this so hang tight)

- **C** (step two) is identifying the **Consequential feelings** and emotions that feel like they are caused by the event. We often think "so-and-so just unloaded on me and called me names and I feel terrible, I feel like crap, and I am angry." Try to list each emotion separately knowing that each emotion is different and carries a different message.

- **B** (step three) The B stands for the **Belief** system that is in place in your mind. As we discussed earlier in this book, emotions are created by the mind—they are not automatic results of situations. The job here is to identify the thought before the thought(s) that are happening just before you feel that feeling. For each of the feelings you listed in C, try to identify the logic statement that is occurring subconsciously (that is you are not consciously aware of them when they happen) in your mind. Logic statements often sound like, "If this . . . then that" and often in a sequence of it/then statements. For example: "If he hasn't made dinner yet, he does not care about me; and if he doesn't care about me, that means our marriage is going down the tubes; and if our marriage goes down the tubes, I will be lonely for the rest of my life. I feel scared, sad and lonely."

- **D** (step four) The D in this process is for **Disputing** the logic in your belief structure. While the person above may have an expectation that dinner is ready, and certainly has a right to feel hungry, it is totally illogical to believe that this is an indicator of marital dysfunction or a precursor to divorce. Likewise, when some tragedy actually happens, of course you will grieve or feel shock or some fear response that your world has been disrupted. But it is illogical to see that as a sign that you should kill yourself or that life is hopeless, pointless, and void of all meaning. So the purpose to this technique is to find the appropriate level of emotion for the situation at hand. By calling out your overdone interpretations and providing a different, more appropriate interpretation of that situation, you will end up with an appropriate level of emotion.

Example: Mike (our ADHD friend mentioned earlier in this book) has temper issues at times. The other day he could not find his screwdriver. The more he looked the more frustrated he became. Frustration became anger and anger became rage until he was storming through the house in such a frenzy that he actually hit a lamp which smashed to the floor. That got his attention and he remembered the ABCD process. He sat down by the broken lamp pieces and started identifying the beliefs that had kicked in. First it was "I never replace things when I use them, I am pissed at myself. I do this all the time—what am I? Stupid? I can't even learn to take care of my own stuff. I am a moron—I am such a loser. I will never learn. This always happens." (Can you see where the rage was sourced?) At the end of the process he was still frustrated that he had not found the screwdriver and upset that he had broken the lamp base, but no longer in a blind rage.

The formula says **Actual** events happen. We interpret them with our **Belief** system. Our feelings are the **Consequence** of the interpretation (not the event). And we have the skill to **Dispute** the logic of those beliefs and turn the emotion back to the appropriate level. Keep in mind that feelings are the result of our thoughts manufacturing the emotion and that *if we have the power to create the interpretation that results in over-the-top emotionality,* *we also have the power to exchange that belief and story with a different one.* What if you had the belief that walls and barriers are there to keep you out? They're there to see how determined you are to get in. How would that change the emotions you felt when you ran into a barrier?

Also—please do not read this as if you should not feel sad when sad things happen or frustrated when you hit an impasse. Those may be the legitimate feelings. But when your feelings stop you or totally destroy your ability to move toward some resolution, then this technique is a real benefit. And we would strongly discourage your use of this technique when you are feeling great, unless of course the appropriate feeling might be grief or sadness. But go ahead and sing "Ding dong the witch is dead!" when it is appropriate!

The clue to determine when you might want to employ the ABCD method is if you feel that your reaction, your emotional reaction, is more intense than the situation would normally call for. You may not be able to see that for yourself at first, but your mate, partner, friends or family will see it immediately. It is important to listen to that feedback.

Integration and Practices – Stretching Your Boundaries

Take a moment to think about your skills and abilities—all of what you can do and know how to do. That list maps out a certain area, a large circle with you standing in the middle. Anything inside the circle belongs to you. But the circle marks the boundary between your skillset and what you are not yet experienced in or skilled at doing. Stepping beyond the borderline is a stretch. Often those stretches are on the continuum of some skill within the boundary. What you are doing is stretching that skill to a new level.

However, sometimes we may take on completely new skills and behaviors. Those are places where the circle is very close to us and trying to stretch out, to push the boundary of our self feels very risky—not because it is a new behavior but because it is so close to home base! Nonetheless, it is just a stretch of the boundary, and our emotional reaction (scared or anxious) is just another of those beliefs firing off the emotion. Perhaps the belief is "I am not like that" or "What if I fail at it?" This might be a great place to apply ABCD and alter the feeling by challenging that limiting belief that is causing it.

But stretching is one of the major tools of transformational change and people who stand as the source and author of their lives. Stretches challenge our mental understanding of who we are or who we aren't, of what we are like and not. Those thoughts are elements of the ego that wants to keep you in place and keep you doing what you know how to do so that you do not experience failure. Ego thinks that failure is bad and will cause undue suffering. But we now know that suffering is transformative, just as love is transformative. Stretching past that discomfort and stretching beyond the point of risking failure will be transformative.

As people who stand as the source of our own lives and our future, we see even failure as a growth point. We see that stretches produce either new skills and experiences or great opportunities to learn. To us there is no "failure." There are either results or lessons, and we welcome the lessons as ways for us to grow. We now see that experience and learning are what we get when you don't get what you expected! Becoming source means welcoming the experience, welcoming and embracing the lessons.

As a result, people who fully own the responsibility of being the author of their future use stretch experiences to accelerate their growth. Rachel is one of those continually growing and stretching individuals who seem willing to step into her fears and do it anyway. When Rachel was a teenager, she had the great opportunity to be a student ambassador to Russia. Rachael had always seen herself as not much of a risk-taker. She was afraid of heights and didn't like things like roller coasters or even Ferris wheels at the park. But while on the trip to Russia, she had the opportunity to visit some medieval sites, one of which was an old castle. However, to get to the castle she would have to walk up an inclined plank that was placed over the moat to the castle wall some twenty feet away. As she stood there frozen in fear, the thought occurred to her that she would most likely never be in Russia again and may never have another opportunity to see that castle. So she took a deep breath and walked up the plank. That moment, she says, changed everything. She still feels fear when she faces a new stretch, but she is confident (having done that many times now) that what lies on the other side of a stretch is a new skill, a new level, and a new way of being that is more confident and effective.

Take a moment to identify your boundaries. List all of your skill categories and then identify a couple of places where you are not as skilled or accomplished as the bulk of your other areas. Let's say you are quite good at many things in your professional area but feel that your public speaking skills are not nearly as polished. Perhaps, if you are like many people, your "enjoyment" of public speaking ranks just above death and chewing shards of broken glass! If that is the case, taking on the area of public speaking would be a stretch.

Identify two or three opportunities for you to stretch your speaking skills. Volunteer to make a presentation on the project update. Then volunteer to speak at the town hall meeting. You might want to join a Toastmasters club and actually learn the art of speaking by practicing several forms like extemporaneous speaking, debate, and oration.

If you feel you lack experience or courage in social situations, take that on. If it is an area of your business or the idea that you might want to launch your own business, identify the stretches that will get you there. But remember, becoming source means that you do not do this alone. Find your team of advisors. Have them help you map out the plan for the launch and the stretches you will encounter. The process of stretching your boundaries never ends.

Shifting States – You Cannot Be in Two States Simultaneously

In the section about "stages and states" we talk about state as the level of your way of being. But we would like to consider a different application of the word state, defined here as your emotional state and the physiological manifestation that accompanies each emotion: anxiety, determination, sadness, frustration, joy, and so on. For example, as you sit and read this, try to take on the posture of someone who is depressed and demotivated. Notice that, in enacting that role, you would lower your head, slump your shoulders, and feel heavy. Now assume the posture of someone who is elated and proud. Here your head is up, your shoulders back, chest is out and you have a big smile on your face. Each emotion has an accompanying physiological manifestation. When you are determined, you lean into whatever you are doing, mentally and physically. When you're aroused, your juices are flowing and your hormones are elevated.

Here's the thing: You cannot be in two different physical and emotional states concurrently. Try it. Look up at the ceiling with a big grin stretching from ear to ear, and try to think of something sad. Either your happiness or sadness will conquer the other, but they will not coexist in the same moment. Your body's neurology and physiology will reflect one or the other. However—and this is a big one—you can use that to your advantage. You can take on the physical state of joy and alter your feelings of sadness. You can engage in something enjoyable and blow those feelings of lethargy out of the room. You can go into the bathroom just before going on stage and do two or three big fist-pumps (with an accompanying "Yessss") to totally erase your nervous butterflies about public speaking. Changing your physical state will alter your emotional state.

Take this on as a routine that can help you regularly. Start by identifying the best positions for a feeling of power or satisfaction. How do you walk when you are happy? What do you do when you win or accomplish some great feat? Catch yourself each time you celebrate, when you are up, and energized. Keep a notebook handy and jot down what you are doing, how it makes you feel, and how you're standing or carrying yourself. Then, when you notice yourself feeling lethargic or stuck, pause and put yourself in one of those positions, and do your celebratory dance.

Many folks we know have several playlists saved for each type of situation. Music has a power to transform your emotional state as well. Pop in your earbuds and get up to dance to your favorite, most irresistible tunes. You will shift in a moment, because you simply cannot be both states at the same time. If you don't have your playlist yet, create one, and have it handy. There are so many great uplifting tunes.

Shifting is a matter of choice. Just as your emotional reaction is a matter of choice, changing your state is as simple (sometimes) as Stop, Shift, Choose!

Section Four

Standing As Source

Kris Girrell & Candace Sjogren

–*7*–

Typhoon Honey

In the introduction, we described Typhoon Honey and why we chose him as the namesake of this book. Typhoon Honey is the source of his life. Yes, he is "just" a tour guide, but we don't think it would matter one bit if his job was to be an accountant, a laborer, or the head of a company. Typhoon Honey would still act the same way and create the same bubble of joy around him. So we would like to leave you with what we believe Typhoon Honey would want to teach us if he were to run a class on how to "be" in this world. We'll call it the Typhoon Honey way!

"Life is rigged in your favor" is one of the main teachings of trainer Chris Lee and it is certainly at the core of the Typhoon Honey Way. Everything that happens is an opportunity. That was the difference with Typhoon Honey. Life does not happen *to him*, he is the cause of everything that happens *around him*. It is his definition of life—life is joy and filled with opportunities to express joy. And so it is. Everywhere he looks, Typhoon Honey sees opportunities to create joy. He also sees suffering and pain every day, since he takes (largely American) patrons to tour the Cu Chi Tunnels and to meet homeless people and craft makers who had been crippled by Agent Orange. But even there, he chooses to see the opportunity to be joy, create joy for them, and greet the travelers (whose ancestors are responsible for this pain) with love and joy.

Typhoon Honey may be unique, but we think not, and we would not be writing this book if we believed that to be the case. So let us pull back the layers of what we call the Typhoon Honey Way. We are hereby promoting Typhoon Honey to being the tour guide of a way to becoming the source of joy in your life. Come along with us as we go on a trip with Typhoon Honey as we imagine it might transpire.

"Mylovemylovemylove," as he would typically begin each conversation, "our first stop on the tour today is the baggage drop!" This is where you leave behind the baggage of what you think you are. Over here you place that big bag called "My self-image and body is who I am." And on this shelf over here, let's drop off the bag called "I am what my external behaviors say about me." "Oh, mylovemylove," our guide says rather gleefully as he wiggles around his oversized body, "this is just where I live, but it is not me!"

"Come, come, over here is the entrance to the ride." The car looks rather scary as it seems to be held together with wire and duct tape. So he adds, "Don't be afraid, it is quite safe. And, myloves, your thoughts and feelings are not who you are either. So step right this way." We climb into the car and it jerks into motion. Typhoon Honey starts navigating the crowded streets and roads a bit too fast and smiles back at us from over his shoulder. "Does your intuition tell you where we are headed? Because as you may now be seeing, your intuition and inner knowledge is not you either. It is just something you have and can use when you wish."

We are beginning to think that Typhoon Honey is perhaps the reincarnation of the Buddha from the way he is talking. And we have no idea how he is driving, as he spends more time looking at us for eye contact when he's talking rather than looking at the road. The road has led us out of the city into the countryside. The bright and rather oppressive sun makes a very clear and visible shadow of our rickety vehicle. "Aha," he giggles, "you see your shadow now. You must remember that your ugly shadow is not who you are either. You will never be rid of it unless you want to hide in the darkness itself. Accepting your shadow is the only way it will be dissolved, myloves. But it is not who you are. And remember, what you don't transform, you will transmit."

The car speeds up a bit more and, given its rather run-down and taped up condition, makes us feel even less safe which seems to delight our guide. "Enjoy, myloves, enjoy! Besides, you are powerless in choosing when you die just as you are powerless in being your separate self. True power comes not from trusting in yourself or your bag of bones and flesh. Power comes from seeing that you have no walls—that you do not end where your skin is." This seems to delight him to no end as he giggles so much that we can't help but join in. Soon we are all laughing and singing—some song that has no lyrics but an incredibly catchy melody.

The singing has a remarkable effect of joining us together. We almost blend together into one being with multiple arms and legs, smiles, and eyes. We sing as one, see as one, and feel as one. "Mylovemylovemylove, you are so much more that you think you are. You are me and I am you, and we are these rice fields and those mountains as well. All things are not separate— all things are one together—one single oneness!" which set off yet another round of infectious laughter.

When we finally arrive at our destination, we park at the foot of a long staircase that seems to go straight up to the sky. Orchids and other fragrant flowers hang from the trees on either side of the stairs. And Typhoon Honey climbs with ease, never seeming to get winded. "Come, come, it's this way," he motioned as we neared the top. We emerge from the stairs to a path that leads out on to the rocky but moss-covered summit. We feel that strange sensation one gets above the tree line where there is nothing to reflect the sound of your breathing. My friend calls it the "headless feeling." Without our noticing it, Typhoon Honey has stripped away all the layers of who we thought we are or thought we were. Not our bodies, actions, or thoughts; not our intuition or shadow or our will. We have become one with everything but there seems to be one more thing our guide had in store for us.

Typhoon Honey sits down in the center of a large circle of stones. He seems to anticipate our question before we asked it. "Mylovemylovemylove, who am I?" And then he almost falls over laughing so hard. He squints his eyes a bit as if to look into our inner being, "I am," is all he says with this beautifully warm smile. "This journey is a journey to becoming 'I am.' From that place you can end the sentence with joy or love or kindness or any of an infinite number of ways of being; because . . . you are." And then he laughs.

Toward an Unprecedented Life

For many humans, life is a relatively straight trajectory; a straight line from birth to death that is relatively predictable based on the experiences and choices we accumulated along the way. Eventually those choices become self-repeating patterns and a self-fulfilling prophecy. We seem to know how this movie will end when we are only half way through it.

But for those who stand as the source of their lives, the future is unwritten and they see themselves as the author to write it. We call this process creating an unprecedented future because the future you are creating has no historical precedent that would determine how the script ends. At any given point in your life you stand at the front end of a huge number of possible paths. Depending upon your choice, any one of those paths might be the one that you end up taking. The problem seems to be that those possible paths are separated by tall hedgerows and we can only see the path that is directly in front of us—not the ones to the left or right, and certainly not the one that is three hedgerows over.

Becoming source means that we can choose which path we take. It simply is a matter of stepping to the left or to the right and looking down the next pathway. And if that is not to our liking, then step left again and continue until you have found the path to your vision. Stepping right or left is just a choice, but it is a choice to move toward *your* future, not the predicted future.

Perhaps you were born into poverty and that seems to be your fate. Or as the elitist economist Thomas Malthus once quipped, "the problem of the poor is their poverty." While that reeks of blaming the victim, the truth is that growing up in poverty affords us less opportunities to get a good education, to afford good, healthy nutrition, or even to be able to relocate to another area where opportunities might be more plentiful. As a result, our state of poverty provides us fewer possibilities and often results in a cycle of repeated impoverishment. I know—that is my history.

It seems to some of us that the hedges on either side of the one and only path in front of us have grown so high and so thick that we cannot see any paths beyond that one. Creating an unprecedented future starts with knowing—deep in your core—that hundreds of paths, down thousands of hedgerows exist. You may not yet see them, but they do exist. Trusting that they do exist, just as surely as the one in front of you now, we step to the right and look again. Step right and look again. But here is the trick to the process:

You cannot keep looking through the same filters and lenses. My lenses that were formed in a world of poverty saw only a world of limited possibilities, a world where there was never enough to go around and one in which each person had to fend for himself in competition with everyone else. And that may be all you can see because that is all that you have ever known. But you can only see what you allow yourself to see. Earlier we talked about the man who married the "money lady." Two people walking down the same street, one of whom saw money everywhere and the other who saw none. Both realities exist in the same time/space continuum. In fact, many realities coexist in your right-here-right-now moment. The question is not do they exist but rather which one will you choose as your current reality for stepping into your new future.

In order to step into your unprecedented future, start with knowing that it is not only possible but that it is entirely within your potential to create. You have all that you need and you will never be more ready than right now. You stop waiting for the conditions to be right, or for the indicators to appear that foretell your success. Success is what you will make when you become the author of your future. Just know that it is yours for the taking!

Your Dream List Revisited

Take a moment to return to the Dream List exercise. Look at the common theme and overarching dream that encapsulates your greatest desires. Ask yourself if this is why you are here—is this why you have been born and what your highest expression can be? Dare to ask yourself that big question. What is your highest purpose? It is not to become wealthy. After all, who wants to collect masses of crumpled green paper? It may not even be that you want the things that the pile of green paper can buy. Your dreams are not who you are any more than your roles, titles, degrees, and accomplishments define who you are.

Write out a list of all the roles you have and look over your resume of accomplishments. Do any of those things define who you are? You could say I am a father, a mother, a good person, a sister, or brother. You could say I am a psychologist or a realtor or accountant. You might say I am healthy or excited to be alive. But in the end, none of those conditions, roles, or actions define you. In fact when you take away all of the ends of those statements what you are left with is simply, "I am!" That is who you are—a simple, pure statement of being—not doing. It is the most powerful statement you can utter and it is even storied to be the name that the Divine called itself when Moses asked "Who shall I say sent me?" The answer Moses heard from the bush was that "I am" is all you need to say!

Recognizing that being is enough—that "beingness" is everything, we can turn to the question of your highest purpose for being. Looking over all of your dreams and the overarching theme, distill out your highest purpose. How are those dreams an expression of your highest purpose? And if they aren't, then what other dreams would you want as a result of "living on purpose"— living as an expression of your higher purpose? Take some time with this exercise—it just might be the most important thing you decide. Of course, if you are already clear of your highest purpose, and once you get clear, it is time to get into action.

The most powerful thing you can do is visualization. We stress two key elements of visualization. First, make your visualization a full "five-senses" visualization. What does it look like? How does it feel? Can you taste it? What smells are associated with it? What would you hear? For example, if you have a goal of owning a house on the beach, visualize the rooms, the view from the deck; hear the waves, smell the salty air, and imagine feeling the sand between your toes. The more details you put into your visualization, the more powerful it becomes. If your higher purpose is, for example, to create a world free of violence, then what would that look like? Would you imagine yourself working with social justice groups, or perhaps conducting seminars for men (by far the higher percentage of violent perpetrators), then imagine getting the training; imagine standing in the circle of men gathered around an outdoor fire, smell the campfire smoke, and imagine what it feels like to know you are making that difference. Visualizing is an essential component of making dreams a reality.

One classic visualization study compared nonathletes visualizing shooting free-throws in basketball. Both groups were asked to shoot baskets and their numbers recorded. The visualization group then spent twenty minutes a day visualizing standing at the free throw line and sinking basket after basket. The other group actually practiced twenty minutes of free throws each day. After twenty days of practice, both groups were tested for their accuracy and shooting ability. The group that practiced actually shooting baskets improved their score by 24 percent, but the group that just used visualization, improved by 23 percent, almost identical to the physical practice group.

The second part of visualization is to actually visualize the path toward that goal. Often people will have a crystal clear vision of their goal or living their highest purpose but fail to achieve that because they have not visualized the process of attaining it. Visualizing the practice, the process of getting there and visualizing handling the obstacles they may anticipate, literally supercharges the visualization process. In research studies when students visualized not simply getting an A on the test, but visualized going to the library, and putting in the time to study, not only did they score higher on the test, they also had lower levels of anxiety when taking the test.

My friend Conor Neill tells about his mentor, Warren Rustand, CEO of Summit Capital Consulting. Conor says that Warren carries in his wallet an old piece of paper on which is a list that his father instructed him to write out when he was just twenty years old of one hundred things he wanted to accomplish in his lifetime. Warren still carries it to this day—and he is nearly eighty years old. It's an old yellow piece of paper written in the hand writing of a twenty-year-old and now protected in a plastic sheath. And Conor says that of the one hundred accomplishments on that list, Warren has achieved ninety-eight of them. The two he has not made were: president of the United States and visit all the known countries of the world (which he is close to achieving). Of the presidency, Warren says that the idea that a twenty-year-old has of what it means to be president does not take into account the stage that it places one's family and that was not something he was willing to subject his family to.

But the really interesting part of Conor's stories about his mentor is that Warren claims that stress does not exist (if you are clear about your values and your vision). Stress only happens when you are not clear. When you know your values and your vision for your life, decisions are easy, and the direction is clear. Having written his vision at twenty has resulted in a life of clarity for Warren Rustand.

Practicing the Basics

In the first chapter we discussed the laws of motion, specifically the third law: For every action there is an equal and opposite reaction. But what does that really mean in day-to-day practice? What we discussed in that chapter was that when we make a declaration for change, we become aware that the universe or at least the part closest to us will show up in opposition with an equally forceful pushback. The harder and more powerful our declaration is, the more forceful the resistance will be. But the third law also feeds into the often-quoted statement by psychologist Carl Jung that "What you resist, persists."

In truth, it persists not through any will of its own, but rather because the resistance we are providing is what manifests the resistance. Just as our declaration into the world caused the world to react in a way that tries to put you back in your place, when we react in resistance to that pushback, we put energy into the system that is pushing against us. It only appears as though it (the universe or whatever) is pushing on us but we are causing that pushback by our act of resistance. But let's take a lesson from the martial arts. In the martial arts, we learn that when any opponent comes toward us with force, rather than resisting it, we allow that advance and use it to our advantage. We use the other person's energy to help us. If someone tries to punch us, we slightly slip to the side and help the punch go by causing an imbalance where the opponent had expected to make contact with us (our face or body for example). We rarely initiate an aggressive move but rather use the other person's energy to our advantage.

Here's a quick way to test this out for yourself. What do you suppose would happen if, when someone or something began pushing against us, we did not resist but rather welcomed the pushback? Try this exercise:

1. Stand firm with your arms extended straight out in front of you and have your partner or friend lean on your hands as hard as they can.

2. Then, abruptly pull your arms back and stop resisting—and see what happens.

3. (Warning) Keep your arms ready to catch your partner because she will literally fall into your arms!

When we stop resisting the pushback, we receive the equal and opposite reaction, that energy comes to us—it falls into our arms where we can receive it, accept it, and make it part of our overall plan. In the poem by Rilke called "The Man Watching," Rilke writes, "What we choose to fight is so tiny! What fights with us is so great. If only we would let ourselves be dominated as things do by some immense storm, we would become strong, too." Learning not to resist, but to welcome the equal and opposite reaction with open arms, we would gain its energy and grow stronger.

After I gave birth to my son, I went into my boss to let him know that I no longer wanted to work the eighty plus hours each week that I was working. I suggested that instead, I wanted to work only thirty-five hours each week. While he said that would be fine, he asked, "What would it take to get your full effort?" I said, "Just asking, I guess." So, I went back to work assuming that I still had to do the greater number of hours but committed in my head to doing something like a thirty-five-hour work week. I hit (in fact, exceeded) my numbers and was able to do as much or more in the thirty-five as I was doing in a far less efficient week of eighty and more hours each week. When I surrendered to my need to be a mom and held fast to my commitment to excellence, I became more efficient—I stopped resisting.

Mastery is not based in learning all of the fancy and complicated elements of life. Like any skill, mastering it comes from thousands of hours spent on perfecting the basics. In the martial arts, Master Jhoon Rhee teaches that there are nine basic movements. All of the fancy skills are composed of those nine movements. You may recall in the movie *The Karate Kid*, that Mr. Miyagi made Daniel paint the fence and sand the floor as ways to gain muscle memory on those nine basic movements.

Likewise, in fully standing as source, it is our willingness to practice those basic skills like enrollment, surrender (nonresistance), integrity, accountability, commitments, stretching ,and so on, that will reap the benefits. Your use of language (the wording you choose) is one of the most important of the basic skills.

Change Your Words; Change Your World

Mastering our thought habits is the basis of all transformational work. But it is in no means a new idea. That your thoughts determine how you will act is one of the oldest principles known to humanity. As early as 800 BCE we see the phrase, "Man becomes that on which he thinks" in the verses of the Upanishads. And in the next century, the wisdom writers, like the writer of the Proverbs, wrote, "Your life is shaped by your thoughts," (4:23) and "as a man thinks, so he is" (23:7). And around the same time the Buddha wrote, "All we are is a result of our thoughts. What you think, you become." Of course, since the time of the sages, there have been many iterations of that precept.

Thus, one of your basic practices becomes the mastery of your language and your thinking. Let's start with replacing some of the real killer words like "must," "should," and "have to," as one of our trainer friends at BBA, Chris Lee, teaches. In their place, substitute any of the following:

- I choose to . . .

- I get to . . .

- I am excited to . . . because . . .

Try it out: on a piece of paper write out as many task-y things you "have to do," "ought to do," "should do," or absolutely "must do," leaving enough space after each one to rephrase it with one of the three alternatives above. Notice immediately how different each one sounds! Somehow, "I have to go to the dentist" sounds like it is worlds apart from "I am excited to be able to go to the dentist."

Spoiler Alert: We know this is a trick. Your brain knows this is a trick. And the entire universe knows it is a trick . . . *and* . . .it absolutely works. Start using choose to, get to, and excited to on a regular basis, and you will absolutely, and unquestionably alter your attitude and your tasks and outcomes. Just like practicing gratitude on a daily basis alters your emotional and mental state, shifting your obligations to choices and blessings will alter your actions as well. There is actually a whole field of psychology called neurolinguistics dedicated to studying the effects of language on the functioning of the brain. So why not give it a try?

While we are at it, there are two other weak words that often run us afoul of our full potential: "want" and "try." The former is a treacherous word because it actually has two meanings. The original meaning of the word want was to be lacking in something. The second definition, more along the lines in which most of us use it today, is to have a desire for something or desire to do something. But it comes from that original meaning that you don't have it to begin with. "I want wealth" literally means that you do not have wealth at the present time and therefore manifests as not having wealth as a reality. Right alongside "wanting" to do something is the term "need to." Try saying either and feeling good afterward. We can't.

Likewise, trying to do something is not doing it. We often ask people in seminars to "try to stand up." Of course everyone stands up until we point out that they are standing up, not *trying* to stand up. Eventually they assume this weird position of slightly leaning forward with their hands on the arms of the chair and legs tensed in a position of ready to stand. Trying to stand is not standing. Trying to improve is not improving. Trying is still in the starting gate but is distinctly not doing, accomplishing, or completing a task. To quote Yoda, "There is no try. There is only do or do not."

Making Commitments And Taking A "Stand"

Earlier in this book we discussed how commitments altered your relationship with the external world. But let's get something straight: There is no such thing as being "overcommitted." If you are committed to more things than you can deliver on, then *you are not really committed to any one of them*. Some of those commitments will be sacrificed—either by default or by decision. Default means that you either run out of time, "bandwidth" or energy, and it just doesn't get done. That is the cheap way out—time should not determine your priorities. Your choices, values, and your vision determine what is important. We all have the same amount of time, but some of us choose to make the most of each moment. We have a saying that if you want something to get done, ask a busy person. Busy people get shit done!

From a position of source, we choose what is not a commitment or to renegotiate those commitments of lesser importance. When you choose to drop the importance on those other actions, you reduce them from commitments to agreements. Your list of commitments is non-negotiable. You are committed to them above all else. Thus, the practice of making and keeping commitments is one that has ancillary skills of setting boundaries and saying "no" to anything that might get in the way of keeping to your commitment. Saying no to a request or to a desire is not only allowable, it is a necessity. However, the rule of powerful, committed people is that every "no" is the result of some committed "yes." Choosing and making a commitment comes with the necessity of choosing *not* to do other things. You cannot have it both ways (for now—in this discussion). Choosing to do X means choosing not to do Y. You do not get to be "overcommitted" in this world of being source.

What, then, determines your commitments in your work setting—especially when and if you are not the owner and chief executive of your business? We often hear of employees who try to push the ownership back on to their boss when they have more work to do than they have time in which to complete them. They often say something to the effect of, "If you want me to do that too, then take something else off my plate." We jokingly refer to this as "upward delegation" and it is a practice we do not ever recommend. There are three elements of the solution we would like to discuss.

First, the answer to what determines your commitments and priorities at work is the scope of work which you are in the position to fulfill. To be certain, that is a moving and evolving target. We don't know anyone who is in a job for which the job requirements are the same as the original job description under which they were hired. Most often, the situation has changed even during the timeline of the hiring process. Work evolves, projects change, and jobs done by employees get to change and grow along with them or be left behind. But the bottom line remains that the first determinant of your work priorities is that which you were hired to do.

The second response in handling extra commitments is the process of renegotiation. This is not upward delegation, however. Renegotiation means looking at all of the commitments together and, starting with the lesser of the important and urgent ones either renegotiate the timeline or the delivery specifications. That might look like delivering half of the work on time and deferring the other half to another time. It might mean trading off pieces of the work to other departments or what we might think of as lateral delegation. It might also involve (remembering that we are the source of all things in our world now) "sourcing" different, better, or other resources to be able to complete those commitments is less time or with less effort.

The third response to the dilemma of too many commitments in too little time lies within. We have become accustomed to thinking and working the way we do because it has always worked for us. But what would happen if you challenged your thought process and challenged the way in which you did your work? What if you used this "overload" situation as a stretch to transform your thoughts and actions?

I was once coaching a group of sell-side: analysts at a large Wall Street investment bank. Having determined the highly complex thought process they used to come to a decision of "buy, sell, or hold," I asked, "Why do you follow that thought stream? Is there a different way of thinking through the process and might there be a more efficient way of sifting through the thousands of data sources required to cover a company stock?" They began looking at each of the decision points in the analytical process. They noticed that in the process of making a decision, there were three parts to the process:

- All information was just information and equal in importance and impact to all other information.

- Patterns of data began to emerge as data was clustered together.

- A hypothesis emerged that was then tested and confirmed as more data was gathered.

The analysts were challenged to conduct an experiment. With half of their cases, they made a decision with only 40 percent of the data in (the point where the hypothesis was formed) and the other half were decided on at the point of 80–85 percent completion. It was noted that the typical margin of error was around 10 percent—or that 90 percent of all the decisions of a top analyst were correct. They tracked the hit rate of both groups and found that the decisions made with 40 percent of the data in were just as accurate as those with full data. What this translated to was that an analyst could make a determination to buy or sell in half the amount of time as the rest of The Street, resulting in substantial financial gain.

Investment analysts are among the smartest people in the world. But as brilliant people they had never challenged their thinking to be different or more efficient because they had always been the smartest kid in class—it worked just fine! The lesson here is that if these brilliant people could greatly improve their thought process (by as much as 50 percent), what might you be able to do if you used your work commitments as a "stretch" opportunity?

Above all of the considerations regarding the determination of your commitments is your "stand." When we came up with the title for the book, *Standing as Source*, we specifically chose the word "standing" for a reason. Taking a stand is taking a position or a perspective that, for you, is nonnegotiable. When Martin Luther King, Jr. spoke, he was not interested in how many "amens" he got or how loud the applause was. After each speech, he would hurry back to his hotel room and see how many people had registered to vote. MLK's stand was that African-American people—as American citizens—deserved to vote without fear of repression. All else was secondary to that stand. Greta Thunberg does not care if people ridicule her as a passionate teenager, or even if they think she has a disability (she has a form of Asperger's syndrome) and outwardly mock her as some news media did. Her stand is for the health of a planet she and her peers will inherit.

Your stand—the commitment that drives your very being—is derived from your vision and higher purpose. Go back to the Dream List and look at your statement of higher purpose. What elements of that purpose are nonnegotiable—as in you will not "settle for" anything less? With that future clearly in mind, craft a "Stand" statement that sounds something like, "I stand for . . ." being as simple and as clear as you can be. Fight the urge to say "I take a stand for" or "I want to stand for," just the pure essential "I stand for (followed by whatever that is for you). Do not mince words; be clear, focused, and precise. My wife, who owns an early childhood education center, has a stand that reads, "I stand for every child's God-given right to a healthy self-esteem." What is yours?

Weaponizing Source

Somewhere in this process, life begins to take on a new luster. You have been through the wringer and have come out the other side shining. Your eyes are clear and you see into things that used to be puzzling or challenges.

Your language has changed from "I have to do this" to I am excited to do it and I choose to do it." What's more, you begin to see that there are others like you who have walked this path of transformation as well. That you are not alone.

It is seductive at this point to part the population into those who are transformed and are practicing this method of living and those who have not. Of course, you may want to surround yourself with those who have. It makes conversations easier because they understand where you are coming from and why you use certain turns of phrases. You don't have to do a lot of paraphrasing and explaining. They get it. But the "they who get it" group is relatively small when compared with those who don't or who have just not been exposed to this way of life, and some of those are people you live with and work with.

Just because you have this understanding and have begun experiencing life on a whole new level does not mean that you have any special rights. If or when you start feeling special and different because you have been practicing this set of life skills, know that your ego is alive and well and trying to play the game of more-than/less-than.

Transformation provides you with no rights. Transformation does not make you special or better than another person who is buried by self-doubt and limiting beliefs. Though you can perhaps see how those beliefs are limiting the other person, it means nothing, especially in comparing yourself to the other person. You cannot preach at them or even tell them that they are missing the boat. You cannot try to instruct them on how to do what you do or how to be in such a way that brings mastery to their life. You can only listen, be curious, and empathize.

It is easy to fall into the reaction of preaching and proselytizing. It is tempting to feel sorry for the other person and for the masses who have not done this work. That is your ego talking. Love has no use for the ego anymore. If you have taken the time to truly understand each chapter in this book, you have likely reached a new level of understanding in your life. By now you are living your life from a source of love and compassion. Transformation has, above all else, ripped out a good chunk of your ego so that you see through that lens of love and compassion. But we are clear that the ego never really dies. All this pity or frustration that the other person doesn't "get it" is just another indication that there is more work to be done inside of you. There always is—transformation is never complete. It is a process, and each day holds yet another opportunity to break down around some new barrier and break through it. Perhaps over time, you just get a little better at moving through the breakdown/breakthrough process.

But, say you live with that other person, or they are family members who may think you are now foreign. You may want to bring them along on the journey—and we will get to that in a moment—but first things first. Because your spouse or brother (or whomever) is far from transforming in the same way you are (careful, that is ego-talk) does not mean you cannot live with them or work with them. Living and working with someone who operates from a set of limiting beliefs, or who does not see any other potential way of being than the one way they have always been, simply is part of your world. It would be no different than reading the news that some difficulty happened or would perhaps be like driving somewhere and coming across a detour. It is part of our world we get to deal with. Because you are learning to be the author of your life does not mean a thing with regard to the other person. We learn in this process that we must meet each person where they are in life, without judgment.

I'm a Fraud

The flip side of weaponizing source is fraud. A fraud is someone who is not living into the life she was born to fulfill. If she was born to be a poet and lives a demure life as an accountant who dabbles in poetry, she is a fraud. If he was born to strive for social justice and knows in his heart that his role is to be out in the fields with migrant workers, but instead is blogging about worker's rights, he is a fraud. We (Kris and Candace) are frauds by that definition. Our station in life is to live into transformation, to experience transformation, and to let ourselves be ripped wide open by the changes that swirl around us and overcome us. Our job is to *be* transformation, to be on the cutting edge of what transformation is, and send postcards back from the front lines.

But *writing about* transformation takes us out of the battle and off the front lines. We are back at base camp observing and writing about what is happening on the front lines, writing about what it is like—not actually experiencing it. We are frauds when we are not there ourselves, all the time. One of Ken Wilbur's best friends is the author David Deida. Deida once wrote an essay entitled "Ken Wilbur is a Fraud," claiming that Wilbur's job was to be a philosopher, to be on the front lines of experiencing life, not to be writing about it. Let someone else write it and report about it! The world needs you, Deida wrote, to be the experience none of us dares to risk.

In that same spirit, we are frauds. I am a fraud when I talk about what has happened and when I write stories about what happened. Yes, that story is true. But relating the story to you is not the same as being the story and being the transforming person in front of you. When either of us stands in front of you and looks into your eyes, you can sense that there is something going on (or at least we hope that). Engaging with you from that place of source—for our own lives and the lives around us, including you—is an experience of transformation. You sense it, you feel the difference.

Writing about this? Well, it is just flaccid, weak, and only an approximation of the real deal. There is no juice in it. not the kind you feel in person. This is not an apology—it is a simple fact. We do not feel shame that we are acting as reporters and journalists. We are in the battle zone, after all, and the things we are reporting are true, for us and for all the people whose stories we have told. We just want to be cognizant that there is a world of difference between talking about transformation and being or living it.

There is the experience, then there is the experience of the experience, and lastly there is the story about the experience we tell others. Take spirituality for example. You may have had a spiritual experience. It could have been a feeling of being touched by angels or as simple as seeing a magnificent sunset that transcends the moment and transports you into some surreal state. The moment of that experience is wordless—it is pure experience. But as soon as you have the experience, your mind wants to place some descriptors on it and classify it so that ultimately you can tell your friends or loved ones what it was like—that is the story about it.

There was a time when I was hiking solo in this eucalyptus forest. The smell was intoxicating on this warm sunny day—when suddenly there was a wind that came up and circled around me. At that moment I knew I somehow was surrounded and being touched by something divine. But when I went to get my camera out to take a picture of this magical place, it occurred to me that nothing could ever capture what I was feeling. I am not even doing justice to the moment as I describe it here. It was pure experience—almost mystical in nature. Perhaps you, too, have been somewhere in the woods at a spot where the sun was slicing down through the trees, illuminating the trail in the most magical way. It was so beautiful that it stopped you dead in your tracks. So you took a picture of it to capture that magic. However, as beautiful as the picture was, when you show it to your friends, it just does not capture all of the magic and wonder of that moment on the trail. There is the experience, the experience of the experience, and the story (or picture) of the experience. This book has been mostly filled with stories of those experiences. Of course they are real and actual events, but we want to be clear that talking about it is not it.

Ultimately our real job is to live it. Our job is to place ourselves smack dab in the face of our fears and our challenges and experience breakdown as a process to get to our breakthroughs.

Enrollment As a Life Skill

When you live with people who have not yet done the work of transformation and who do not yet understand what it means to be source, it is natural to want to bring them along. Doing so is a process called enrollment. Enrollment has a bad rap in some social settings. It often sounds like sales or preaching—and it is not! Enrollment is the process of opening up another person to seeing their future and realizing their dreams and aspirations. We all have dreams. For some people those dreams have been lost or packed away under layers of hurt or disappointment. Enrollment is enrolling them into their life.

Enrollment starts with your vision of your friend. What beauty or what brilliance do you see in them (even if they don't)? You cannot approach enrollment from a place of wanting them to bridge the gap or change for you. Enrollment has nothing to do with you and your wants and desires. All you need to do is be clear that you see the possibility in them. From that perspective you will want to invite them into the conversation. This is a heart-to-heart conversation of the love you see in them, the magnificence you see in them. It is based on how important this person is as a relationship. Obviously, you can enroll a relative stranger just by engaging them quickly in their vision of the future. But when it comes to your spouse, your loved ones and family, we feel too enmeshed in their history or their difficulties to maintain a perspective supportive of enrollment.

Inviting your friend into the conversation is as simple as asking if the two of you can talk about their dreams. You have known this person for some time now and you have heard their heart's desires in many conversations. It's time that you have a heart-to-heart conversation about what those mean to them. At this point you become an advocate for their dreams. Help them see— really see—the dream coming true. What would it look like? What would it feel like? What would be possible then? Bring it to life and support them in reigniting the fire. Support them in seeing that this is not just "possible." it is what is meant to be and what they desire most in life.

When you have gotten your friend excited once again about their desires and dreams, enrolling them in this way of being is as simple as letting them know that you have a path that will get them there. Whether that path is enrolling in reading a book like this, or participating in a program or course or following some coaching from you, connecting your friend with their passion makes taking the next step of committed action rather simple. Obviously, we are advocates of one of those action paths called the Boston Breakthrough Academy, but there really is only one transformation path as taught by a number of centers around the world. What matters is giving your friend the keys to drive that vehicle.

Enrollment is more than just getting your friends on a path of transformation. Enrollment is a life skill. Everything—getting a loan to buy a house, interviewing for a job, selling something, speaking in your church or temple—literally everything in life starts with enrollment. Without enrollment, you are bound to be playing life as a lone wolf. So when you are enrolling your friend in some path of transformation, their receptivity and urgency is a great measure (feedback if you will) of (1) how they view the depth and quality of your friendship and (2) how well you have enrolled them in their vision.

Getting a new job is also a measure of how well you have enrolled the company in (get this) their vision of what they want. Getting a job is not about your credentials, not about your resume bullet points, and certainly not about what your recommenders say about you. It is their job, their desk you will sit at using their computer, parking in their lot, and the check that is signed over to you will have their name on it—not yours. Getting a job is not about you. It is about their needs and desires, and as such, getting hired is enrollment. Just like enrollment in transformation, getting hired is enrollment in their vision. But when you show up as enrolling instead of showing up as wanting to get something from them, you will place yourself in a very small and select group who are focused on what the company is focused on—and that differentiates you from all the other applicants who have a similar skill background as you. The same is true of relationships, intimacy, starting a company, or whatever you have next in life. Everything in life is enrollment.

Outgrowing Friends and Blowing Up Relationships

One of the most difficult developmental steps that one makes in their own personal journey is taking an inventory of existing relationships. There are certain people in your life who just aren't going to be able to or refuse to make this transformational journey with you. It Is not a happy topic but certainly one that churns up a lot of emotions. It becomes particularly difficult with your closest friends and lovers. Just writing these words feels heavy.

When we form relationships, we do so in the context of a certain stage of our lives, as a persona or the person we were at that point. Thus, the other person in that relationship obviously sees in you some aspect that they want as a completion of their sense of self, or as a friend, or partner. We like someone because of the qualities we see in them and because those qualities fit with the type of life and socialization we wanted for our lives at the time when we first connected. That in itself is not a problem. But when we move away from that personality or character that we once had, it alters the original precepts of the relationship. While that does not have to be a problem, it can become one for many of us.

Take, for example, a marriage relationship. Many people fall in love with the person they first see and hope to be in relationship with *that* person for the rest of time. That gets challenged as each person expands and grows in different roles: parenting, education, maturing, and so on. If our marriage is codependent on that other person fulfilling a certain role, then our world is shaken up when they no longer fulfill that role for us. It is imperative for healthy relationships to have room for each person to grow and change. Relationships that do not have that dynamic partnership based in growth fall apart or get into deep ruts of programmed behaviors. In a committed relationship, we get to learn to let go of our prescriptive belief about how the other person "should" be and move to a place where we love them for each iteration they become as they grow, blossom, and mature.

However, there are relationships we have with others that are not growing, where you simply have outgrown the relationship. You may have gotten into this relationship or friendship long ago when you were immature or prior to your stepping onto this path of transformation. Then you began to grow and let go of old beliefs and dysfunctional behaviors. As you continue on this path, it becomes clear that these other people hold onto a way of being that is no longer compatible with yours. You may have had a circle of friends that included someone who was just plain negative. For them life is a problem and there is always a complaint. In the group they had been tolerated simply because they had always been that way and (perhaps) you all had just grown up together.

There may come a time in these situations when associating with a stagnant person or negative grouch no longer serves you and, in fact, seems to pull you down. At that point we have to face the painful decision of letting go. This could be as simple as unfriending them on Facebook, but usually it is more complicated. It becomes a matter of having to "blow up" the relationship. Blowing up a relationship is a bit like the process of clearing a broken agreement that we discussed earlier. First of all you can't just walk away, not so much because it is not fair to the other person, but because you are not creating closure for yourself. Just walking away leaves a "back door" open for your mind to wander out and get twisted around on, and, in many instances, is the "easy way out."

Blowing up a relationship is also not just a "fuck you" moment of blowing up *at* the other person. It should be done in a humanistic and loving way that leaves the other person with a sense of dignity. First of all, schedule some time to talk it through. Then when you get together or have that call be straightforward and clear. Don't take time with small talk and beat around the bush. Tell the other person that you are on a personal journey, that you are shifting and growing toward a new future. Then let them know that when they do a specific behavior, it impacts you in such a way. Own your reaction and say that is something you prefer not to do in your new way of living. If you feel that there may be hope for future changes in the other person, then tell them that as long as they persist in doing that, you will need to break off the relationship. It is your choice and based on what you need.

But if you sense that this person is committed to their way of being and that there is little possibility for change, just leave it as the fact that you need to move on and that will mean that you will not be in communication with them any longer, and that you wish them well. Do not apologize; do not backpedal your position. You may be the first person to be pointing out this behavior on their part and/or it may be the first time it actually landed.

It is important to note that by labeling the behavior and not the person (not who they are but what they do), you allow them the opportunity to alter that behavior and change. You may not feel comfortable with a face-to-face meeting or even a call, in which case you may wish to write a good old-fashioned letter. However, we strongly recommend against the use of email or text for this action. Not only will it not work, it can set you up for some retaliatory actions that can interfere with your work and life. Be clear: Treat the other person with respect and dignity and come from a place of caring for them irrespective of the harm they may have done to you. As source, you have the power to choose to be gracious even in blowing up a relationship.

Monitoring Your Inner Opponent

By now the world has become your mirror. You have learned that if you want to see your progress, you need only look around and observe the results and relationships in your life. But there is more to this mirror than just monitoring your results. The world—life in general—is a reflection of what is going on inside of you. Previously we mentioned that the martial arts teaches that we have only one opponent—ourselves. The same is true in the world of source. Every challenge you encounter is not a result of some naturally occurring phenomenon. To the contrary, if it appears as an obstacle, the thought called "obstacle" is your mind's interpretation of the situation. And it is seen as a challenge only because your mind still believes that you either do not have the capacity (or talent or resources) to do it or you are not enough (strong enough, fast enough, rich enough, smart enough).

When you encounter this opposing force, your new response is now joy and elation! It is seen as a good thing not because of some machisma/ machismo, but rather, it has given you the opportunity to expose and uproot another of those limiting beliefs that have held you back all these years. You now view it not as in the way, but instead as the way **in**. Barriers are not there to keep you out, but rather to see how intent you are on getting in or through.

So the work on identifying and monitoring your inner opponent is purely self-work. Self-work—at least the kind that leads to self-worth— is a set of disciplines: meditation, journaling/ reflection, proper nutrition (including limiting alcohol and junk foods but including plenty of hydration), and exercise. You choose to become a spiritual warrior, a warrior of self-management and self-determination.

The key metric of how well you are mastering this work is your ability to shift away from the habitual response and into the new and transforming path. In fact, it is not just that ability to shift that is the metric, it is how long it takes you to "get off it" and shift to your chosen way of being. As you practice being present, as you practice standing in abundance, and as you practice loving unconditionally, you will get better and faster at the art of shifting.

In your journal, write out the goals and intentions you set for each of the areas of your life:

- **Mental Health**. What are your educational goals? What books are you intending to read this year? Are you taking a class or getting a certification? How much time do you want to spend daily or weekly on exercising your mind? How determined are you to never stop learning? What worries you? Where is your "scary" edge and where does your shadow hide?

- **Physical Health**. How much do you want to weigh? What is your ideal? What foods are you eliminating? How much exercise are you committing to—get specific in the number of times per week, the amount of time and the type of exercise (walking, bicycling, swimming, jogging, yoga, martial arts)? How determined are you to building and maintaining a healthy body and a vital sexuality?

What beliefs do you hold about your age as it concerns your physical health?

- **Spiritual/Emotional Health**. What is your gratitude discipline going to be? What type of meditation, contemplation or spiritual practice are you committed to? What are you committing to give to others (time, money, volunteerism)? What questions do you not wish to ask or fear trying to answer? What power is greater than you? How do you learn humility?

- **Relationship Health**. What are your goals for your relationship? If you are not in a committed relationship, do you want to be in one? Who do you want to build or repair relationships with? How is your relationship with your family of origin? What new relationships do you want to develop at work, in your community, in the world? Who are you enrolling in taking a greater stand in their lives? What relationships do you avoid? How does that reflect your inner opponent?

Ethics and Meritocracy

There is an ethical responsibility one assumes in taking on this life and in being source. We recognize that we have assumed a certain set of powers and conditions that are not universal. Many who might be otherwise powerful and successful contributors to their world may not have been gifted with the set of circumstances or privileges that we often take for granted. There are people whose circumstances are so debilitating that it may seem nearly impossible for them to rise out of their conditions. We would consider ourselves as insensitive were we to step over the conditions of those who are disenfranchised, disabled, exploited, un-banked (having no bank account or means to save money), or victims of systemic injustice. These issues are human issues and by default are our issues as well. As we contend with the abundance of the universe, that sharing in abundance carries with it the responsibility of being a channel of abundance for all and that we cannot win at the expense of others' losses; we likewise are required to be part of the solution for the disparity of justice and humane conditions for those who are often forgotten. We consider this a matter of ethics and accountability.

Recognizing privilege is difficult—it is like trying to differentiate some parts of the air we breathe from other parts. Privilege shapes our language, is the foundation of the logic and philosophy that guides our thinking, is endemic in the principles of psychology we feel are "normal," and is the context in which most people who read this book function. Privilege is a product of power, and the power that those who are privileged to possess can shape destiny, frame our lives, and even to select or limit resources to accomplish much of what we would consider just conditions for living.

My life partner Sarah has an avocation of empowering women. For years she has worked with women, designed and run trainings, and led women's organizations at the local, regional and international level. Frequently she would be coaching some woman on the phone, and one time I noticed a different tone to her conversation. When she hung up, I asked her what that was about, and her response surprised me: "She feels like prey in her relationship." Not understanding, I asked what that meant. Sarah explained that most women feel like prey. They have been ogled, pinched, groped without consent, and whistled at all their lives—they just feel like prey, she explained. The thought had never occurred to me. As a six-foot, three-inch athletic male, I have never once had the feeling of being prey—not even walking home after rugby practice at night in Central Park, New York! That is male privilege. But whether we talk about privilege as male privilege, white privilege, economic privilege, geographic privilege, or any other unconscious state of life that set us even a step ahead of our sibling humans, our duty is to become aware and wake up to how privilege has tilted the scale.

When we stand as source, we also own the responsibility that we are source for the suffering of others who live without those privileges. You cannot have it both ways: being source and ignoring a third of the world's population who suffer. We are either source or we are not. Choosing to live as the source of our lives means that we choose to participate in the whole of life, and by extension, that we are the source of life for others as well. If we have any hopes of holding on to the gifts that we generate in standing as source, then we own the responsibility of sharing those gifts with others. After all, our gifts were given to us to be shared—that is the nature of abundance. When we hold onto something as "ours" or "mine," we stop the flow of abundance and lose any chance of understanding greatness.

Somewhere in the conversation of abundance and privilege, we encounter the egoist concept of merit—a belief that we deserve (whatever it is we think we deserve) because we worked for it.

The extension of that same principle is that if the disenfranchised of the world were to work hard enough, they would be inheritors of this same level of abundance. Nothing could be further from the truth nor more bound up in ego and privilege. It is not simply a matter of pulling oneself up by the bootstraps for the disenfranchised. Entire systems (economic systems, justice and legal systems, social, political, and even geographic systems) are working to hold them down. If humanity can share in abundance, humanity also shares in pain, wealth disparity, injustice, and exploitation. Becoming source carries with it the ownership of balancing these imbalances. We recognize that we are all part of the same universal system and as long as even one human suffers, all of humanity is suffering. Thus, we do NOT hold the idea that "I deserve" what I get and "if only they would work as hard," they would earn these rights as well.

There was a YouTube[22] video that became popular showing a teacher trying to illustrate the effects of privilege. He had all of the students start on a baseline in the field to have an opportunity to get a one hundred dollar bill he was holding. The first one to reach him would win. But then he added some conditions. If they lived in a home with both parents, they could take two steps forward. If they never had to work to help the family out financially, they could take two more steps. If they did not have to count on a scholarship or athletic ability to get into college, take two more steps forward. And he continued that way as the privileged students moved closer to the goal. Some looked back at those still on the baseline who remained motionless, heads down, looking dejected. Finally, he said "go" and one of the foremost of the privileged students easily grabbed the money. And many that still stood at the baseline never even attempted to run in the race. After the exercise,

---

22 "Privilege/Class/Social Inequalities Explained in a $100 Race," YouTube, October 14, 2017,

https://www.youtube.com/watch?v=4K5fbQl-zps

the teacher debriefed the students on what they learned. The race had been rigged from the start. That is the effect of privilege.

Meritocracy is a term used to describe an attitude that one gets what one earns. It comes from a northern European work ethic that holds that if you work hard enough for anything, it can be achieved. But meritocracy also holds the thought of entitlement. Those who work hard enough are entitled to reap the rewards. But the foundation of meritocracy is scarcity and competition; not abundance. It assumes that we all have the same starting point and the same innate skills. Meritocracy does not take into account centuries of poverty, malnutrition, lack of access to education, or even to clean water. And those are just a few of the inequities that wealth disparity and privilege have created as the starting block for our disenfranchised siblings in the human family.

Psychologists usually discuss this thought (merit and entitlement) under the general heading of "locus of control." When we are doing well, we see things that happen in our favor as within our span of control—"I did that!" It is referred to as an internal locus of control. Conversely, when we experience "bad luck," we see those instances as outside of our control—"It happened to me!" This is referred to as an external locus of control. Meritocracy is based in the conversation of locus of control in as much as people who ascribe to the principle of merit believe that they have control and can positively affect their outcomes through their effort. They have mottos like "no pain, no gain" and "God helps those who help themselves." Yet despite this, because meritocracy is a locus of control principle, they also hold fast to the belief that "shit happens" and that forces outside of your locus of control have power to disrupt their path. "You just have to hunker down and work through it," they will say.

So what are we to do? The day Andrew proposed to me we started talking over dinner and he began enumerating the woes of the world. It quickly spiraled downward to this heavy and sad place. My immediate response was, "So what can we do?" His answer of essentially that there was nothing we can do had me reconsidering my earlier "yes." But I said if we think we can't do anything, then what are we here for? Why are even alive if not to be part of the solution? That discussion began our journey toward creating this center of BBA and the life we are now living as partners.

As transforming people who totally accept our being source, we also get to accept our complicity in the injustices that create systematic disenfranchisement of others. We see our complicity in the plight of the disenfranchised and we own doing our part to work for justice. But like the other issues in our lives that require our attention and understanding, being source carries no guilt within it; it only requires our shifting to source a different outcome. If we approach working with people who are living in poverty or those who society has demeaned, from a place of guilt, we are still coming from a place of us/them. It is only when we are in full solidarity with our oppressed siblings and stand beside them as one of us that we can act in full power with them.

My friend, an ordained minister, traveled to Standing Rock Reservation during their protest of the Dakota Access Pipeline. Her intentions were purely to be in support and add her body and voice to that of the Standing Rock Sioux tribe. But when she arrived, the council informed her that she could work in the food preparation or in any of the many duties required to support those who were protesting, but she would not be permitted to stand on the front line. The elders said that because she did not know what it is like to have been oppressed for generations and still stand in nonviolent protest, they feared she would get angry or indignant at how the military was treating the protesters, and as a result be a disservice to their nonviolent stand. Her lifetime of privilege and power would result in her experiencing oppression in a way that was inconsistent with their values. Imagine for a moment how committed to peace it would be for those who have been oppressed, murdered, and cheated for hundreds of years to continue to work peacefully for the right reasons. So, seeing that truth, she supported their efforts as best she could from behind the scenes.

Brazilian educator Paulo Freire (in his now-classic text *Pedagogy of the Oppressed*,[23]) identified five different perspectives or experiences in working with poor (which Freire defined as those who are powerless, dismissed, or considered as lesser by society) people. These are not sequential or progressive levels of understanding, but rather different awarenesses we must move through to get to full solidarity.

---

23 Paulo Freire, *Pedagogy of the Oppressed*, 30th Anniversary Edition. (New York: Continuum International [now Bloomsbury Publishing], 2008).

1. The first perspective is feeling compassion for people living with injustice and as a result befriend them. Seeing exploitation and suffering, we are naturally moved to compassion. My family and I were helping a family living in dire poverty clean up a trashed section of their house so that they might rent that part out to others. The place had not been lived in for several years and was filled with trash, rotting garbage, and dog feces everywhere. At lunch my son sat down with me and said, "Dad, I'm embarrassed at how disgusted I am with the conditions they live in. It is not right and I know that is my privilege speaking, but they are people and they deserve better than this." His heart was breaking for this family and yet all we could do that weekend was clean and repair the building.

2. The second perspective of solidarity is indignant anger at the injustice, the place where our friend perhaps was when she wanted to support the Standing Rock tribe. We see clearly the bitter injustice of these exploitive systems and are outraged at the suffering they cause.

3. The third perspective of solidarity seems a bit like patronizing. Freire says, as we move into solidarity, we may tend to idealize the virtues we see in oppressed peoples. We often hear people who have worked in so-called "third world" locations saying how happy and generous the people were, that they have little or nothing to give but will give you anything they have. When Andrew and I went to Vietnam, we encountered this phenomenon. We wept at the war memorial, but we experienced no resentment or hostility from the Vietnamese people there. Our guide, Typhoon Honey, simply explained that those atrocities were done by other people, not us. It was both humbling and inspiring. Another version of this level is to admire people's stamina for dealing with the oppression, calling them strong or thinking that someone is almost superhuman to work three jobs, keep a house, and raise five children in such conditions—or for Andrew and me to think of the Vietnamese people as more evolved.

4. The fourth perspective is disillusionment with those we are trying to help. This is almost the opposite of the previous perception of "superhuman" when we become upset with oppressed people's defeatist attitude. People who have lived in oppression and have been told countless times that they are nothing, that they will never amount to anything and have no value, often internalize those thoughts as an acceptance of failure, like the students left at the starting line in the one hundred dollar bill game. They become convinced by their surrounding culture that they are nothing and worthless and lose all will to even try. To outsiders, they may appear lazy and like they are using the system to get a free ride. Freire says we need to confront *our* disillusionment, resulting from *our* attitude, and not something wrong about them.

5. The fifth perspective is to actually walk with the oppressed as one of them and to allow their perspective and living conditions to transform us. Freire says that it is not until we are able to say "we poor" or "we oppressed" that we are in full solidarity with them. It is one thing to work with poor, oppressed, and exploited people yet have the ability to escape to our homes and "normal" way of being. But when we actually let it in and let those conditions penetrate our inner world, the forces of oppression have the ability to transform us, to feel a deeper level of compassion, not based in pity, but in understanding firsthand what that suffering is.

This fifth level of awareness is not something we can easily hold on to. Like being totally present in the moment when our minds are continually sifting through past, present, and future, living in solidarity is difficult and challenging. Andrew and I moved into an apartment in Roxbury to be in solidarity with the poor and destitute of Boston. We made friends with homeless people and some of the addicts on the street corner. We invited them to breakfast. But in no time those same people we were befriending were continually knocking on our door asking and demanding that we give them something or feed them more and we slipped quickly back into the fourth level of disillusionment and resentment. It is not easy, even if this is your life's calling.

Lest we think that this only applies to the world of wealth disparity and hunger, we want to be clear that this same conversation can be had with society's discrimination and disenfranchisement of others based on human sexuality. Our gay, lesbian, gender neutral, transgender, bisexual, polyamorous, or otherwise queer siblings in the human race have long suffered much of the same disenfranchisement and oppression as do people of different races and skin colors or economic standing. Oppression is oppression. We get to be allies to with the disenfranchised.

My daughter is an ordained minister and identifies as queer because she is married to a transitioned man. The level of maturity that both my daughter and son-in-law can teach me is so advanced *because* of having to ask and answer far more questions on life, on who they really are and what their identity really is. As a large, white, heterosexual man, none of those issues were ever challenged in my life. Wherever you are on the continuum of life and economics, there is always someone who can teach you more.

Many of the principles and practices outlined in this book cannot be simply handed to people living in oppression. Without an understanding of the psychology of the oppressed (what is called Liberation Psychology) we can miss the mark or come across as uncaring and uninformed. Without the proper humility, *Typhoon Honey* will not land well with others. While we talk about the power of declaration, our understanding of that power starts from a position of privilege and freedom to choose in the first place. We still get to contextualize these principles so that they fit within the culture and paradigm of the people we are enrolling. Stepping into leadership for a person of color in a culture of discrimination is not simply a matter of "saying so." It is imperative that we be taught first by our oppressed sisters and brothers and learn to approach transformation from their starting point, not ours.

My primary care physician is a brilliant doctor, and her husband is a wealth manager for a major brokerage firm. While engaging in normal chit-chat at the end of a physical a few years ago, she mentioned that she and her family were planning where they might be able to go for summer vacation—so many places were not safe. When I pointed out that the travel alert level was lower than it had been in a few years, she said, rather bluntly, "Kris, look at me! My skin is brown—and brown is the color of terrorism. People don't see my degrees when they look at me; they see a brown-skinned woman with a brown-skinned man and two brown boys! There are few places we can go in the world where that is not the case, and that's scary." If that is the case for an affluent American doctor, imagine the level of oppression felt by those whose skin color is Black or Brown or Yellow, or for people who don't look like they have any available cash reserve, people who are gender neutral, transgendered, or whatever their particular natural state might be. And those are issues in our country—a place considered by much of the rest of the world to be a place of affluence and freedom.

Our ability to stand humbly beside the oppressed ones, to walk with the poor and know life from their perspective, is essential before we are able to "teach" the skills of transformation. We first get to learn from our queer friends what life and sexuality really means; from our exploited sisters and brothers what suffering is; and to experience hunger not as a choice to fast but as a daily condition of life. Then, when we are transforming by that experience, when we understand the starting point of living with oppression, we can begin to frame the perspectives of becoming source differently for them and for ourselves. As we are fond of saying, there is always more, and tomorrow is a much bigger day!

Playing Full-Out

In this new and transforming way of living, we discover a new level of energy and a new capacity for getting stuff done. You may notice people who seem to accomplish far more that others and we would contend that those folks are not smarter than the rest of us but rather that they know how to maximize their efforts. They know how to work in harmony with (and not struggling against) the laws of the universe. They understand how their minds work and the role of limiting beliefs, and they work consciously to eliminate their limiting beliefs. They understand how to tap into abundance (of everything from financial to resources and even time) and become part of the flow of abundance. And most of all they have learned how to play "full-out."

Prior to doing any transformational work, we lived more or less as a victim of the forces around us. Our fears and limiting beliefs prevented us from taking that leap of faith and the first step on a new path. We may have thought of ourselves as fully in the game of life but we were fraught with struggles and barriers that seemed, at times, to be insurmountable. So our best efforts fell way short of our dreams, goals, and visions. We felt like we had to "muscle it" through our difficulties. But when we removed those limiting structures and began working in harmony with others and the forces of the universe, when we cleared the path of our own obstructions, we were able to play full out.

Playing full-out is engaging in life with all of our faculties. We pull out all the stops, we open up the throttle on life's engine and go at each endeavor with mindful presence and positive enthusiasm. Each day and each encounter is entered with a "bring it on" type of attitude. We have gratitude not only for our blessings but for everything (including life's disasters) that comes our way and have a learned optimism for how it will turn out. We look at each moment in life as an opportunity to say "YES!"

My parents used to tell me a story when I was a child. They said there were these twin brothers who baffled their parents because one was so pessimistic and the other, with the same experience, was so optimistic. So they took the boys to a team of psychologists to see what could be done. The psychologists put the two boys in different rooms for observation. The pessimistic boy was placed in a room filled with every popular toy they could find and the optimistic brother was placed in a room full of horse manure! Fifteen minutes later they went to check on the boys, only to find the one lad sitting in the middle of the floor crying his eyes out. When asked what was the matter, the boy sobbed, "Wouldn't you know it, with all these toys here, the one I really wanted to play with isn't here."

Panicked, the psychologists feared the worse for the other brother and rushed down the hall to the manure room. But when they got there, they found the boy laughing and singing and throwing globs of manure up in the air as he moved around the room. "What are you doing, boy, why are you laughing?" The boy looked up and laughed, "Looking for the pony," he said, "With all of this horse poop here, there has to be a pony somewhere!" Transforming people are eternal optimists. Like the second boy, they look for the pony in everything. They see possibilities (not probabilities—but what is possible) in every situation. And they do not and will not stop until they make those possibilities a reality.

As transforming people, we play full-out because we can. We play full-out because we no longer fear the worst but rather expect the best. We play full-out because we no longer feel held back by our self-imposed constraints. And when we experience obstacles and constraints from the outside world, we welcome them as ways to learn coping and dealing with those. We play full-out because we know that we are part of making the whole system, the world around us, and the world at large more functional because of our involvement. We play full-out because it has become who we are.

What's Next?

This book does not get to end here. The next chapters, however, will be written by you. You are the undisputed and sole author of your future and you absolutely get to be the source of your grand story. To launch you on this next phase we suggest you take a moment to practice the following visualization exercise.

The Perfect Day: Sourcing Your Future

Find a comfortable place with no chance of interruptions for the exercise, then read through this completely before actually creating the visualization. Better yet, record yourself reading this section or ask someone else to read it to you so that you can close your eyes and fully visualize.

Breathe deeply to relax your body—taking several rounds of deep long inhalations and slow, relaxing exhales. Imagine waking up in the most perfect place. Imagine the sun streaming into the room. The window is open and you can smell the clear air—is it the clear air of a mountain retreat or the fresh smell of an ocean breeze? Whatever it is, it is your favorite scent. Notice what you hear. Do you hear birds chirping or maybe the waves rolling in and other sounds of nature gently waking you up?

As you roll over in bed, you are waking up next to the most perfect person. Who is it—is it your spouse or lover or maybe your child? Perhaps it is a mirror looking back at you to see that you are the perfect person to wake up with. And so, you rise to make that perfect breakfast, just the way you like it, and as you turn on some music, your favorite song is playing, and you dance around the kitchen. And you smile—this is going to be a great day!

You decide to go out for the day—a stroll or a jog or bike ride, or maybe you take a leisurely drive to that perfect spot to spend this day with your perfect person. When you arrive, every person that has ever mattered to you is there, smiling and they just can't wait to spend time with you. Together you have the most perfect day doing all those things you all love to do—all afternoon and into the evening.

As the sun starts going down, you all bid farewell and head back to your perfect place. You feel absolutely fulfilled and get ready for bed. Laying your head down on the pillow, you exhale a sigh of pure contentment at the close of your perfect day.

Take time to flow through your visualization and allow your fantasies and wishes to run the vision

Think over your perfect day. Where did it take place? What was the best part? What is it that you have gotten clear as something you definitely want to create as part of your future—your heart's desire?

Write down the elements of your perfect day. Write out what is clear about your future. Start telling others about your future and tell as many people as you can. As you continually tell the story, your details will get clearer. The more you tell it, and the clearer it gets, the more powerful your power of sourcing and manifesting it becomes.

Dream Manager

Many companies and their employees have used the Gallup survey, and while it is often misunderstood and under-applied, the survey found some critical information about employee engagement. Essentially Gallup surveyed over two million employees in the US asking two simple questions:

1. About how much effort does it take for you to execute well on your functions?

2. Of the remaining amount of your energy (which they named "discretionary" energy), what would it take for you to want to give that to the organization?

The answer to the first question averaged out to be just around 80 percent of the employee's effort is necessary if completely fulfilling their job requirements. The results of what would get people to give their additional 20 percent discretionary energy were interesting. Beyond the usual thoughts like having peer relationships at work, many of the other forces that would elicit discretionary engagement had to do with how well the work related to the employee's higher purpose and their dreams for themselves.

Australian consultant Matthew Kelly wrote a book called *The Dream Manager*[24] that explores this concept to the fullest. Working with hourly workers and low-level employees (often the least engaged in their work), Kelly found that when he asked about people's dreams and focused on keeping their dreams alive, the workers were more engaged and productive. Not only that, but they were inspired by their coworkers' dreams and actively participated in helping them achieve them and keep the vision alive. Every year he brings the whole company together for a dream session and asks each person to bring one hundred dreams (short term, in the next five years, and beyond five years). He gets groups talking and sharing about their dreams, and he says, "out come the pens," because the listener gets excited about another person's dream and wants to adopt it as well. But the really powerful effect Kelly says is that after he does a dream session with his employees, all he can think of is their dreams. They might be talking about a project and he finds himself thinking of that person's Dream List and how he might help her realize that.

People are human and they are most human when their body and soul are engaged. Dreams live in your soul, not in your head. We have asked you to dream throughout this book, and we have asked you to envision your future, write down your dreams (have a hundred dreams), to be like Warren Rustand and carry it around with you until you've checked off every one of them. It doesn't matter how old or young you are; you get to have dreams. In fact, the older you get, the more important those dreams become. Elderly people waste away most often because they falsely believe that they can't create and live into new dreams. However, those who do have dreams seem forever to be young and energetic.

Typhoon Honey is a book about personal empowerment—empowerment to be the author of an unprecedented life. It starts with understanding the world around you and within you and is driven by your dreams. "What's available for every single person who is on this path to leadership is that we

---

24 Matthew Kelly, *The Dream Manager* (New York: Hyperion/Beacon Publishing, 2007).

get to continue to be students of life, for life." (Michael Strasner) Never stop dreaming, and never, ever doubt your power to manifest those dreams as reality.

You are the source.

Works Cited

1. Barrett, Lisa Feldman. *How Emotions Are Made: The Secret Life of the Brain.* New York: Houghton Mifflin Harcourt, 2017.

2. Brennan, Barbara Ann. *Hands of Light: A Guide to Healing through the Human Energy Field.* New York: Bantam Books, 1988.

3. Buck, Jotina L. *Change Your Language, Change Your Life: 30 Enlightenments to Unlock Unlimited Possibilities.* CreateSpace Independent Publishing Platform, 2015.

4. Chapman, Gary. *The 5 Love Languages: The Secret to Love That Lasts.* Chicago, IL: Northfield Publishing, 1992-2015.

5. Emoto, Masaru. *The Hidden Messages in Water.* New York: Atria Books, 2006.

6. Freire, Paulo. *Pedagogy of the Oppressed,* 30th anniversary printing. New York: Continuum International [now Bloomsbury Publishing], 2008.

7. Gerdeman, Dina. "Minorities Who 'Whiten' Resumes Get More Interviews." Harvard Business School, May 17, 2017. https://hbswk.hbs.edu/item/minorities-who-whiten-job-resumes-get-more-interviews.

8. Girrell, Kris. *Wrestling the Angel: The Role of the Dark Night of the Soul in Spiritual Transformation.* Andover, MA: Kindle Direct Publishing, 2015.

9. Hanh, Thich Nhat, *The Heart of the Buddha's Teaching: Transforming Suffering into Peace, Joy and Liberation.* New York: Broadway Books, 1998.

10. "Project Implicit." Harvard University. https://implicit.harvard.edu/implicit/takeatest.html

11. Kelly, Matthew. *The Dream Manager.* New York: Beacon Publishing, 2007.

12. Kurtz, Ernest and Katherine Ketcham. *Experiencing Spirituality: Finding Meaning through Storytelling*. New York: Jeremy P. Tarcher/Penguin, 2014.

13. Lombardo, Michael and Robert Eichinger. *FYI: For Your Improvement: A Guide for Development and Coaching*. Minneapolis, MN: Lominger Limited, Inc., 2004.

14. Pressfield, Steven. *The War of Art: Break through the Blocks and Win Your Inner Creative Battles*. New York: Black Irish Entertainment, 2002.

15. Radin, Dean, Nancy Lund, Masaru Emoto, and Takashige Kizu. "Effects of Distant Intention on Water Crystal Formation: A Triple Blind Replication." *Journal of Scientific Exploration* 22, no. 4 (2008): 481-493.

16. Saad, Layla F. *Me and White Supremacy: Combat Racism, Change the World, and Become a Good Ancestor*. Napersville, IL: Sourcebooks, 2020.

17. Sinek, Simon. *Start with Why: How Great Leaders Inspire Everyone to Take Action*. New York: Penguin Publishing Group, 2011.

18. Strasner, Michael. *Mastering Leadership: Shift the Drift and Change the World*. New York: Direct Impact Publishing, 2018.

19. Zander, Benjamin and Rosamund Stone Zander. *The Art of Possibility: Transforming Professional and Personal Life*. New York: Penguin Publishing Group, 2000.

Videos

1. "Dr. Quantum – Double Slit Experiment." YouTube. December. 27, 2010. https://www.youtube.com/watch?v=Q1YqgPAtzho

2. Gates, Bill. "The Next Outbreak – We're Not Ready." TED2015, March 2015. https://www.ted.com/talks/bill_gates_the_next_outbreak_we_re_not_ready?language=en

3. "Perception: Inverted Vision Experiment Clip," YouTube. July 25, 2013. https://www.youtube.com/watch?v=MHMvEMy7B9k

4. "Privilege/Class/Social Inequalities Explained in a $100 Race." YouTube. October 14, 2017. https://www.youtube.com/watch?v=4K5fbQl-zps

5. "What Is a Fractal (and What Are They Good For)?" Khan Academy. https://www.khanacademy.org/partner-content/mit-k12/mit-k12-math-and-engineering/mit-math/v/what-is-a-fractal-and-what-are-they-good-for

Select MSI Books

A Guide to Bliss: Transforming Your Life through Mind Expansion (Tubali)

A Theology for the Rest of Us (Yavelberg)

A Woman's Guide to Self-Nurturing: How to Build Self-Esteem by Being Nice to Yourself (Romer)

El Poder de lo Transpersonal (Ustman)

How My Cat Made Me a Better Man (Feig)

How to Get Happy and Stay That Way (Romer)

How to Live from Your Heart: Deepen Relationships, Develop Creativity, and Discover Inner Wisdom (Hucknall)

How to Stay Calm in Chaos (Gentile)

Old and on Hold (Cooper)

Puertas a la Eternidad (Ustman)

Rainstorm of Tomorrow (Dong)

Roadmap to Power (Husain & Husain)

Seeking Balance in an Unbalanced Time (Greenebaum)

The Rose and the Sword: How to Balance Your Feminine and Masculine Energies (Bach & Hucknall)

The Seven Wisdoms of Life (Tubali)

Weekly Soul (Craigie)

What Readers Say about *Typhoon Honey*

"*Typhoon Honey* blows your mind with gale force winds. Kris and Candace succeed in connecting the essence of life into a parable of drip-feed stories with the science to back it all up. This is a must read for anyone wanting to level up in their life."

Andy Chaleff
Mentor, speaker and author of *The Last Letter* and *The Wounded Healer*
Amsterdam, Netherlands

"Reading *Typhoon Honey* is like taking a personal journey into the deepest parts of yourself and discovering a roadmap to your brightest future. Girrell and Sjogren offer the perfect blend of story-telling, practical lessons, and plenty of opportunities for purposeful reflection. But it's not like other books in the "self- help" genre. Bring your pencil and paper – prepare for an active commitment to yourself. It is SO worth it!"

Amy Bladen-Shatto, Ph.D.
I/O Psychologist and Director of Global Leadership
WL Gore & Associates
Dover, DE

"From working with Kris and Candace for years and seeing their commitment to transformation take form in this text, I can say firsthand that *Typhoon Honey* is worth the read. If you have ever wondered whether all you have dreamed of in life is possible, you'll want to take notes and apply the lessons in *Typhoon Honey*."

Michael Strasner
Transformational coach and trainer
author of *Mastering Leadership* and *Living on the Skinny Branches*
Colleyville, TX

206

"This intriguing book is written by two master coaches who have put the exercises in this book into practice in real organisations for many years. It is important for leaders of organisations and for the people they lead to clarify their vision and purpose. This book gives practical tools for organisational leaders to live and lead with intention. It is wonderful to see Kris and Candace sharing their wisdom and tools to a wider audience through this book."

Conor Neill
President, Vistage Spain
Professor of Leadership, IESE Business School
Barcelona, Spain.

"INCREDIBLE - *Typhoon Honey* starts the reader on a personal journey with all the coordinates turned on - intellectual, visceral, emotional. We can't help but discover ourselves, understand ourselves, and accept ourselves in the process, and become prepared to shape our futures with a new outlook. The authors are true to their word...everything *is* connected."

Stacy Feiner, Psy.D.
Business coach and author of *The Talent Mindset*
Cincinnati, OH.

"Sjogren and Girrell are quite simply an inspiration. Their work and writing help us gain a true understanding of what it means to be the source of our results in life, not the product of them. Their promise is to help us not only create real results but to leave a lasting impact on the world."

Omri Dahan
Chief Revenue Officer, Marqeta, Inc.
Oakland, CA.

CPSIA information can be obtained
at www.ICGtesting.com
Printed in the USA
BVHW040814020222
627782BV00010B/784